SECOND EDITION

Reading, Responding, and Writing

Short Essays and Stories for Composition

W9-BEC-198

SECOND EDITION

Reading, Responding, and Writing

Short Essays and Stories for Composition

DOMENICK CARUSO
STEPHEN WEIDENBORNER

St. Martin's Press, New York

Senior Editor: Cathy Pusateri
Editor: Karen Allanson
Associate Editor: Elayna Browne
Project Manager: Denise Quirk
Text Design: Gene Crofts
Cover Design: Jeannette Jacobs Design

For information, write:
St. Martin's Press, Inc.
175 Fifth Avenue
New York, NY 10010

ISBN: 0-312-03604-3

Acknowledgments

"Without Emotion," by G. Gordon Liddy. Copyright © 1980 by G. Gordon Liddy. From the book *Will* and used with permission from St. Martin's Press, Inc., New York, NY.

"Good News," by Robert Fulghum. From *All I Really Need to Know I Learned in Kindergarten* by Robert Fulghum. Copyright © 1986, 1988 by Robert Fulghum. Reprinted by permission of Villard Books, a division of Random House, Inc.

"A Fling on the Track," by Bill Cosby. From *Love & Marriage* by Bill Cosby. Copyright © 1989 by Bill Cosby. Used by permission of Doubleday, a division of Bantam Doubleday Dell Publishing Group, Inc.

"Rolf," by Sylvia Ashton-Warner. From I *Passed This Way* by Sylvia Ashton-Warner. Copyright © 1979 by Sylvia Ashton-Warner. Reprinted by permission of Alfred A. Knopf, Inc.

"Henri," by George Orwell. Excerpt from *Down and Out in Paris and London*, copyright 1933 by George Orwell and renewed 1961 by Sonia Pitt-Rivers, reprinted by permission of Harcourt Brace Jovanovich, Inc. Reprinted by permission of the Estate of Sonia Brownell and Martin & Secker Ltd.

"Father," by Langston Hughes. Excerpt from *The Big Sea* by Langston Hughes. Copyright © 1949 by Langston Hughes. Renewal copyright © 1968 by Arna Bontemps and George Houston Bass. Reprinted by permission of Hill and Wang, a division of Farrar, Straus and Giroux, Inc.

"Our English Teacher," from *North toward Home* by Willie Morris. Copyright 1967 by Willie Morris. Reprinted by permission of Joan Daves Agency.

Acknowledgments and copyrights are continued at the back of the book on pages 237–238, which constitute an extension of the copyright page.

PREFACE

Any instructor who has questioned the mechanistic and prescriptive approaches of most composition textbooks—and who is ready to trust students' natural curiosity and their desire to communicate—should find this reader challenging and refreshing. *Reading, Responding, and Writing*, Second Edition, aims to involve students with reading selections to a greater degree than traditional textbooks allow. Prompted by reading selections and by student responses to them, students are encouraged to express their personal concerns in writing. They are motivated to improve their reading and writing skills by learning about themselves and discovering their interests and concerns.

Our approach in this book grew out of our efforts to apply reader-response methods in the classroom. Finding it impractical to follow a "pure" response model under typical classroom conditions, we have adapted the individualized aspects of the method so that students themselves guide each other through discussion and peer editing. They begin by recording their strongest responses to a reading selection, without being guided by preconceived rhetorical or thematic categories. Then, by sharing their responses and getting classmates' reactions, they identify a topic and thesis they care about, and they develop their ideas into a first-draft essay. During revision students again are guided by peers' reactions, and perhaps by the instructor as well, so that the finished essay effectively expresses the point of view they developed in response to the reading.

The Introduction to *Reading, Responding, and Writing* immediately involves students in the process just described. Besides orienting them to this personal approach to reading and writing, the Introduction provides practice in the various classroom procedures that make it work. After the introductory chapter, the book offers four thematic sections of readings: Responding to People, Responding to Situations and Events, Responding to Ideas, and Responding to Language. The first four readings in each of these sections are followed by sample responses and questions about the responses to help students focus their own ideas. The last selections in each part appear without sample responses or questions, as do the Additional Readings in Part Five; students have been prepared for these sections by their work with the guided readings. Finally, Part Six, Improving Your Writing, can be used at any point during the course, either to introduce or to review the main concerns in developing a thesis, drafting the essay, and revising it.

In this second edition, as in the first, we have paid special attention to providing readings that will serve as springboards for student responses. In this regard, we have taken the suggestions of our reviewers seriously. We would like to thank Bob Cosgrove, Saddleback Community College; Dan Gallagher, Laredo Junior College; Darrel Hagar, Salisbury State University; Joe LaBriola, Sinclair Community College; and Margie Whalen, San Antonio College, for their careful reviews of the text. Thus, in line with their suggestions, we have replaced a number of readings from the first edition with new selections that should effectively broaden the reader-response potential of the text.

Whether you adhere to the methods described in the Introduction or combine them with your approaches, we believe that the provocative readings and sample responses in this book will result in an active, spontaneous classroom in which students will be challenged to participate—and will take pride in their achievements.

CONTENTS

PREFACE   v

Introduction   1

   HOW TO USE THIS BOOK   1
     Examples of Responding   2
     A Warm-Up Exercise   4
     Reading, Responding, and Writing: An Overview   5

   SAMPLES OF READING, RESPONDING, AND WRITING   7
     "Mary and Mrs. Brown," Evelyn R. Fulbright   8
     Sample Responses to "Mary and Mrs. Brown"   12
     From First Response to Complete Essay   14
     Peer Responses: Constructive Criticism   17
     Considering the Second Draft   23
     Other Responses, Other Essays   24

   A REVIEW OF THE PROCESS   32

PART ONE

Responding to People   35

   Without Emotion   36
     G. GORDON LIDDY
       Sample Responses 37/Considering the Responses 40

   Good News   42
     ROBERT FULGHUM
       Sample Responses 43/Considering the Responses 45

   A Fling on the Track   47
     BILL COSBY
       Sample Responses 48/Considering the Responses 51

   Rolf   52
     SYLVIA ASHTON-WARNER
       Sample Responses 53/Considering the Responses 55

ADDITIONAL READINGS _____

Henri   58
  GEORGE ORWELL

Father   59
  LANGSTON HUGHES

Our English Teacher   61
  WILLIE MORRIS

The Slanderer   63
  ANTON CHEKHOV

PART TWO
_____

Responding to Situations and Events   67

  You Should Have Been a Boy!   68
    ELIZABETH CADY STANTON
        Sample Responses 70/Considering the Responses 73

  Salvation   75
    LANGSTON HUGHES
        Sample Responses 77/Considering the Responses 79

  Unresolved Grief: Drowning in Life's Debris   81
    SUE PATTON THOELE
        Sample Responses 82/Considering the Responses 85

  A Real Loss   87
    FERN KUPFER
        Sample Responses 88/Considering the Responses 91

  ADDITIONAL READINGS _____

  Your Eyes Can Deceive You   92
    ARTHUR BARTLETT

  There's Only Luck   94
    RUTH REICHL

  Growing Up in the Shadow of an Older Brother or Sister 97
    SALLY HELGESEN

The Story of an Hour   100
KATE CHOPIN

PART THREE

Responding to Ideas   103

Intelligence   104
ISAAC ASIMOV
Sample Responses 105/Considering the Responses 108

No Allusions in the Classroom   110
JAIME M. O'NEILL
Sample Responses 112/Considering the Responses 115

What Makes Some Things Wrong?   117
HAROLD KUSHNER
Sample Responses 118/Considering the Responses 120

Reflections on a Hockey Helmet   122
GREGORY BAYAN
Sample Responses 124/Considering the Responses 126

ADDITIONAL READINGS

How about Low-cost Drugs for Addicts?   128
LOUIS NIZER

Problems and Pain   131
M. SCOTT PECK

The Young and the Old   133
KONRAD LORENZ

The Boy Who Drew Cats   135
LAFCADIO HEARN

PART FOUR

Responding to Language   139

Small-fry Swearing   140
SUSAN FERRARO
Sample Responses 143/Considering the Responses 145

Words as Weapons   147
RICHARD MITCHELL
    Sample Responses 149/Considering the Responses 152

Children's Insults   154
PETER FARB
    Sample Responses 155/Considering the Responses 157

Parallel Speaking and Real Conversation   158
THEODORE ISAAC RUBIN
    Sample Responses 158/Considering the Responses 161

ADDITIONAL READINGS ⎯⎯⎯⎯⎯⎯⎯⎯⎯⎯⎯⎯⎯⎯⎯⎯⎯⎯⎯

Talking Like a Lady: How Women Talk   162
FRANCINE FRANK and FRANK ANSHEN

How Fathers Talk to Babies   164
BARRY McLAUGHLIN

Saying It May Make It So   167
JOHN C. CONDON, JR.

The Test   169
ANGELICA GIBBS

PART FIVE
⎯⎯⎯⎯⎯⎯⎯⎯⎯⎯⎯⎯⎯⎯⎯⎯⎯⎯⎯⎯⎯⎯⎯⎯⎯⎯⎯⎯⎯⎯⎯⎯⎯⎯⎯⎯
Additional Readings   173

What's in a Name?   174
LOIS SWEET

How Cocaine Took Control of My Life   176
TONY ELLIOTT

Television: The Plug-in Drug   179
MARIE WINN

Punishment versus Discipline   184
BRUNO BETTELHEIM

The Mirages of Marriage   188
WILLIAM J. LEDERER and DONALD D. JACKSON

The Pursuit of Loneliness 190
PHILIP SLATER

Males Just Born Gross—Humor Them 193
STEPHANIE BRUSH

The Darkness After 195
ED and LORRAINE WARREN with ROBERT DAVID CHASE

How to Stay Alive 198
ART HOPPE

The Monsters in My Head 200
FRANK LANGELLA

Labor 203
RICHARD RODRIGUEZ

A Nigerian Looks at America 209
T. OBINKARAM ECHEWA

Thumbs Out 212
STEVE SPENCE

PART SIX

Improving Your Writing 215

GETTING STARTED 216
From Topic to Thesis 216
Selecting Your Thesis 216/Stating Your Thesis 218/
Developing Your Thesis 219
Drafting the Essay 219

REVISING YOUR FIRST DRAFT 223
Example 1 224
First Draft 224/Instructor's Comments about First Draft 225/
Revised Draft 226
Example 2 229
First Draft 229/Classmate's Comments about First Draft 230/
Revised Draft 231

A CHECKLIST FOR READING, RESPONDING, AND
WRITING 235
Reading 235
Responding to Reading 235

Writing   235
      Selecting and Developing the Thesis 235/
      Drafting the Essay 236
Responding to Writing   236
Revising the Essay   236

GUIDE TO AUTHORS AND TITLES   239

SECOND EDITION

Reading, Responding, and Writing

Short Essays and Stories for Composition

Introduction

HOW TO USE THIS BOOK

This book will improve your ability to communicate in nonfiction writing. We want to emphasize the word *ideas* and point out that we are not concerned with teaching creative writing, such as poetry or fiction, or with showing you the proper forms to use for business letters and reports. Instead, the assignments in this book ask you to develop your own ideas into essays that will be clear and effective, essays that your readers will understand and appreciate. The key to becoming an effective writer is, first of all, to come up with an idea that you really want to express. This book will make you aware of some specific ways to discover ideas that are important to you and to develop them into effective essays.

We could, of course, ask you to sit down and "think of a topic that is important to you," but most of our students found this to be one of the most difficult assignments of all. Maybe the first ideas that come to mind are too personal (a family problem, perhaps) or too "heavy" (preventing nuclear war, or achieving social justice). Or maybe too many ideas pop up at once, making it difficult to choose the best one. At any rate, most writing courses make use of essays or literature and ask students to analyze these as models for their own writing. Assignments in such a course often require the students to write about the same topic as is found in the model or to imitate the form of the model.

This book does provide readings for you to consider, but we ask you to respond freely rather than to analyze them, and the writing assignments do not require you to imitate the forms of the readings. Furthermore, you will be asked to respond not only to the reading selections but also to each other's writing. This reading-responding approach calls for a good deal of active participation, but the interaction between you and your classmates can improve your writing more quickly than an approach in which you must work entirely on your own. By getting feedback from your classmates during the writing process, you will discover what has gone wrong in your writing, or at least what can be improved, *before* you have to prepare your final draft. In addition, by sharing your responses to *other* students' work, you will learn to analyze and criticize writing in general. This, too, will make you a better writer.

You may wonder exactly what we expect when we ask you to "respond." Basically, within each reading we want you to find some idea, large or small, that evokes a strong reaction in you. Whatever that reaction may be, you will be asked to respond by writing down your ideas so that they can be shared with other student writers. The goal is to discover a topic that you care about. Don't try to guess what the instructor is looking for or what your classmates are likely to think. Even if you think your response may come out of "left field," if it represents something meaningful to you, it may well be worth pursuing as a topic for a paper.

Responding, of course, is a natural part of being alive. We do it all the time, but usually our responses take the form of thoughts or conversation. In this course you will simply record those responses in writing. Let's look at a few examples to show you what we mean.

Examples of Responding

Four college friends who thought they might sign up for a journalism course attended a meeting at which the instructor described the course. Briefly, this is what he said:

> **Professor:** I am looking for intelligent, perceptive students who feel deeply committed to producing a newspaper that readers can respect for its ability to tell the whole story, clearly and without bias, in an appealing style. The paper should be so good that people will feel they have missed something vital any day they fail to read it. I hope you are all fine writers, but if you're too good, I'll have nothing to teach you. At any rate, I am not looking for an Edgar Allan Poe or a John Updike. I want people to be able to read the paper rapidly or at leisure and still come away feeling they have been as well informed as they expected. In this course, you will be required to write something for every class, including one polished article per week, which will be submitted for my comments. Grades will depend primarily on what you get out of the course, for I assume you are all capable of doing the work competently. I am looking forward to getting to know each of you personally and watching you develop your talents in this most exciting field of work.

The four friends met afterword and shared their reactions to the presentation:

Betty: I like this guy. He seems to be more interested in students than in teaching us all the boring details of printing and the history of publishing. I remember all the pressure trying to get a newspaper out in high school, and I sure want someone who cares about me to be there when all the hassling starts.

Sal: It sounds like too much work to me. Can you imagine writing three papers a week? On top of all our other classes? No way!

Betty: He didn't say "three papers a week." He just wants one article, and that probably wouldn't be as long as an essay in your history course. The other writing isn't even turned in, and it might be quite short. Besides, we're supposed to *like* writing.

Dan: He reminds me of this guy I had in high school—same little glasses and peculiar way of thinking. Was he ever nasty when it came to grading! No one could tell what he was looking for.

Janice: I know what you mean, but he seems very sharp to me. He probably has very high standards, but that's what I'm looking for. If I'm going into journalism, I want a teacher who knows what he's doing.

As you can see, people's reactions can come from very different directions. Although some people might not think that a teacher's looks should stop anyone from enrolling in a course, life is filled with such surprising responses. And they are in no way meaningless to those who experience them. What seems like too much work to one person may seem like a worthy challenge to another. Indeed, if all people *did* have the same responses, there would be no reason to write in the first place.

Another example of how people respond differently involved the same students and a decision regarding a photograph proposed for the front page of the college newspaper. The photo is on page 4.

Betty thought the photo was too gruesome, that it would give the paper an image of pandering to ghoulish interests, as horror movies do.

Janice disagreed, saying Betty had missed the point—that the shock effect might save someone's life, since people would think twice before driving recklessly or when drinking.

Sal allowed that the photograph might serve a good purpose, but he objected to putting it on the front page, where news items and the issues of the day should be presented.

What do you think? Does this photograph belong on page 1 of a college newspaper? Take a moment right now to express your opinion briefly in writing.

Caraballo/Monkmeyer Press Photo Service

A Warm-Up Exercise

Before showing you how a sample assignment works, which will entail reading a complete essay, let's warm up by responding to the following newspaper article:

Mrs. Ivory McInnes, 38, of Greenacres, Kentucky, after having been reported missing by her husband, Ira, six days earlier, showed up at the state police barracks in Wolfsboro, Tennessee, explaining that she had been abducted by alien beings, who were operating out of what seemed to be a spaceship. Ennis Air Force Base officials acknowledged that on the night Mrs. McInnes disappeared they had received several reports of strange lights in the sky within a 50-mile radius of Greenacres. Mrs. McInnes said she was walking back home alone from town a little before midnight when a dimly glowing circular aircraft, about 40 feet in diameter, landed vertically in a field about a mile from her house. She was so stunned that she fainted, only to wake inside the craft, which she sensed had taken off, although she had no sense of motion. The figures of the aliens were not distinctly defined in the eerie light of the ship. She could understand them but does not recall whether they spoke aloud. They began asking general questions about the various kinds of life on this planet and about her species' way of life. Most of their subsequent questions dealt with science and technology. When they realized she could not answer these questions, they returned her to land, though not at the same point they had picked her up. Wolfsboro lies 130 miles southeast of Greenacres. When interviewed on their farm, Mrs. McInnes's husband, Ira, offered no comment when asked about his wife's adventure in space.

Record your response to this story right now, in one or two paragraphs that express whatever ideas or feelings it raised in you.

Reading, Responding, and Writing: An Overview

From the preceding examples and warm-up exercise, you can see that, indeed, you respond to stimuli all the time, and very often your responses are unique. Even when you basically agree with the opinion of others, the way you express that opinion and the intensity of your feelings about it are unique.

Many people have little trouble *saying* what they think, and they usually can make other people understand them—even if they have to shout or repeat themselves. When it comes to *writing*, however, people sometimes find it difficult to share their ideas clearly. In conversations we get feedback from our listeners and can tell when they lose interest or disagree with what we're saying. But writing is usually done in isolation, without readers at hand to tell the author when an idea or opinion or phrase goes over their heads. This book is designed to provide feedback to writers in the form of readers' responses. You and your classmates will share your ideas (1) about reading assignments, (2) about each other's responses to those readings, and (3) about each other's essays. In this way the necessary link between writers and readers will be forged, allowing you to learn firsthand how your written ideas are received.

Throughout this book the practice of reading, responding, and writing will lead you to identify your strengths and weaknesses in writing. The entire process is detailed in the next section, but you should know at the outset what to expect:

- First, you will begin each assignment with a reading selection, to which you will respond briefly in writing.
- Then you will share your strongest response about the reading with your instructor and classmates—in class discussion or small groups or by trading your paper with someone else.
- Next, you will give and get feedback by talking with your peers,

whose responses will help you to adjust and clarify the ideas you
are developing into a paper.
- At that point, you will expand your ideas into a first draft,
  which again will be shared with peers.
- After another round of discussion, you will select the best ideas
  your classmates have shared, and you will use them to revise
  your draft into a finished essay.

Before deciding that this process sounds frightening or tedious,
consider two thoughts. First, your classmates are in the same situation
as you; since everyone is subject to the process of sharing and receiving
feedback, no one escapes criticism—and everyone will learn to offer it
helpfully. Second, although the pattern of reading, responding, and
writing will be repeated throughout the course, the readings you will
respond to and write about are all very different. If one reading fails to
inspire you, the next one may really spark your interest and have you
writing in a frenzy. In addition, within each major part of the book, the
readings are related; you may find yourself returning to an earlier
reading because a later one presented a different point of view, and
you want to consider the two together.

Finally, the first four readings in each part are followed by sample
responses written by students in an actual class. The questions we raise
about those responses should get you started on the right foot by
making you think a little more deeply about your own reactions to the
readings. The combination of your own responses, your classmates'
feedback, and the sample responses should make you reach for a pen
with enthusiasm.

Now let's practice the process we've outlined by going through
a sample assignment, complete with students' responses, feedback ses-
sions, and resulting essays.

SAMPLES OF READING, RESPONDING, AND WRITING
(How *Some* Students Have Used This Book)

Now that you are familiar with this book's approach to writing, let's practice the general process that you will follow throughout the course. The best way to demonstrate the process of reading, responding, and writing is to take you through a sample assignment. We will begin with a reading selection and some sample responses of students in a class much like your own. Then we will see how these students developed their responses into an essay through peer editing—by reacting to each other's work and sharing their ideas.

Like the students in this example, you should record your response to an essay as soon as you finish reading it. In this way you are likely to express your strongest ideas, the ones that are truly important to you. Rather than writing a summary—which is unlikely to express what you think about the ideas in the essay—try to respond without deeply analyzing the reading selection. Avoid trying to guess what your instructor may be looking for; *your response* is all that matters at this point. By recording your own thoughts about the essay, you will discover a topic that truly interests you. Then you can develop that topic into a full-length essay by trying out your ideas on classmates, friends, and your instructor.

You may find it difficult at first to let yourself go and record your impressions in writing. Buy don't worry. You will catch on quickly, and soon you will respond freely and naturally—in class as well as on paper. An important part of this process is to compare your responses with those of other readers. That's why we provide sample responses to the first four reading selections in each part of the book.

Now let's look at an actual classroom example of reading, responding, and writing. After you have read the following essay, record your strongest response to it by writing a short paragraph. Then compare your response to the reactions of the four students in this sample classroom.

Mary and Mrs. Brown

EVELYN R. FULBRIGHT

It was Valentine's Day. I had just walked into a classroom to observe an experimental reading class. A girl with sparkling eyes caught my attention, mainly because she was larger than the rest of the children and because she had a big valentine on her desk.

Then it all came back—the classroom many years earlier when I was a preservice teacher, the place where I had learned one of my most valuable lessons about helping children with behavior problems. It was a lesson that symbolized a child's need for love and self-esteem—but that is getting ahead of the story.

Going back to that time, I recall that my professor had assigned my class to observe in elementary classrooms. I was to be with Mrs. Brown's first grade class.

The professor had given us all check sheets to record our observations and verbal instructions for marking them, but I was still scared—afraid that I would not see what I was supposed to see. Exactly what I was supposed to see, I did not know. My fellow students seemed equally vague about our purpose.

With pencil and paper in hand, nevertheless, I sat in a corner of Mrs. Brown's room, looking as hard as I could, anxious to observe some special secrets of teaching and learning. My eyes came to rest on Mary, who was larger than most of the children. Later I saw on Mrs. Brown's records that she was repeating first grade.

As the days passed, I noticed many things about Mary: that her desk seemed too small for her angular body, that her clothes never seemed right—one day they were too big, the next day, too small. Wrinkles were always evident, and what seemed to be a favorite blue sweater had all the buttons missing.

In spite of her unkempt appearance, I was drawn to Mary. She was a pretty child, with naturally curly hair—the kind I had always wanted. Unfortunately, it was seldom brushed. Her eyes were bright and flashing—sometimes friendly, sometimes mean. On cold mornings, her chapped cheeks looked almost as if she had gotten into her mother's rouge.

Mary couldn't read very well, but she drew beautiful pictures, and I 8
saw her slip them onto the teacher's desk.

One day I happened to be observing at recess, and I saw Mary give 9
her meat sandwich to a stray dog. I wanted to commend her for that,
but I pretended not to notice because she yelled, "I dropped my sandwich." Still I knew what she had meant to do, and I was glad.

Some days, however, I would hear Mary say threatening things as 10
she walked a few steps behind the other children. If anyone laughed,
Mary seemed to be pleased.

For weeks she seemed to torment one student in particular, a girl 11
named Jean. I even saw her knock Jean down and then pretend she
had done so accidentally.

After that happened, I watched Mrs. Brown talking to Mary with 12
her arm around her. I remember wondering why Mrs. Brown didn't
do something more drastic.

Looking back on my own school days, I remembered my teachers' 13
taking immediate action against such offenders. That had certainly
seemed right at the time.

Then the holidays came, and I forgot about Mary. When I re- 14
turned to the classroom, she was wearing the same blue sweater she
had worn all year. When Mrs. Brown wasn't looking, some of the children made fun of Mary's clothes. That afternoon when I went to say
good night to Mrs. Brown, I found her busy with Mary and a package.

On my next visit, Mary had on a different sweater, which appeared 15
to be new, and her hair was brushed that day. She was smiling. Her
eyes were bright and happy.

But it was not to be Mary's day after all. The mother of another 16
child, Betty, called, and the principal delivered a note to Mrs. Brown
that said Mary had been picking on Betty on the way home from
school. I sat back to see what Mrs. Brown would do this time.

Just before the dismissal bell, I heard her ask, "Mary, will you be 17
able to stay a few minutes? I've got a lot to do and I need help."

"Yes, Ma'am," Mary grinned. 18

Out of the corner of my eye, I saw Betty's face brighten as she got 19
her books ready to go home.

But another day, as three o'clock drew near, I saw a mean-eyed 20
Mary mutter something under her breath. I also observed the frightened face of Jean. I looked to see if Mrs. Brown noticed. As the bell
rang, Mary smiled unpleasantly, again, and Jean hung back as Mary
ran out the door.

Then I saw that Mrs. Brown was getting ready to go out. She called 21
to me, "I'll be back in a minute. I have some things I want to go over
with you."

I peered out the window and raised the sash a bit. Sure enough, 22 there was Mary, standing on the playground and waiting for Jean, who was walking very slowly in her direction.

Then Mrs. Brown appeared, and Mary looked up at the teacher, 23 chewed on the corner of her lip, and shivered. Mrs. Brown knelt down, put her arm around Mary, and smiled just as she smiled when she was very happy in the classroom. She brushed back a lock of Mary's hair, and I heard her say, "My, your hair looks pretty today. I want to tell you before you go home." Then she spoke quietly, still smiling at Mary. She buttoned Mary's sweater up right.

Quite often Mary looked away when anyone talked to her, but this 24 time she looked right at Mrs. Brown, blinking her eyes rapidly. I again picked up what Mrs. Brown was saying, "I know I can count on you, Mary." Then she hugged Mary and waved goodbye.

I waited for Mrs. Brown. I wanted to ask her about Mary, but I 25 didn't want to admit I had listened. Anyway, I noticed that she was smiling as if she saw something I couldn't see, so I said nothing.

Some days later I saw Mary and Jean eating lunch together. After 26 school they went off, laughing and talking.

Then it was Valentine's Day. Everything in Mrs. Brown's room 27 seemed to be covered in lace and red hearts and cupids. The children had decorated individual mailboxes for themselves.

All the children put valentines in one another's boxes. I distributed 28 mine too; for some reason, I "mailed" the prettiest one I had to Mary.

After the other children had read all their valentines, Mary 29 reached into her box and pulled out her last one. It was so big and so pretty that the children murmured "Oh's" and "Ah's" when they saw it.

It was truly the most magnificent valentine of the day. On the in- 30 side under the verse, the sender had printed in big letters, "Dear Mary, I love you," but whoever it was had not signed the card.

Mary let the other children hold the card and smell it. It had a 31 delicate fragrance, which they liked. Mrs. Brown smiled approvingly.

In the days that followed, there seemed to be something different 32 about Mary. Her hair was brushed; her "new" sweater was buttoned. She had a ribbon in her hair, and her shoes were shiny.

There was more. Mary smiled a lot and offered to help Mrs. 33 Brown. She read aloud with more expression, and Mrs. Brown called on her often.

I never let Mrs. Brown know that when I was in the card shop 34 buying my valentines, I saw her buy the big valentine Mary had received. I had been curious about why she was buying such an expensive card.

I hoped Mrs. Brown knew I was getting the lessons she was teach- 35 ing me. We never discussed them.

At the end of our classroom observation course, the professor 36
asked, "What was the most significant idea that you have gained from
this course?" I responded, "Teachers must be sensitive to the hurts and
needs of children. Children respond more positively and learn in a
more effective fashion in such an environment." I did not explain
about Mary and Mrs. Brown. At the time, it was not an easy story for
me to tell.

Over the years, I have shared bits and pieces of the story with pre- 37
service and in-service teachers in various ways, but it has been many
years since I thought of the details.

Not until I walked into the reading classroom that morning and 38
saw the large girl with the big valentine on her desk did I remember
the story as it had happened. That is what stirred my memories and
prompted me to wonder whether this reading teacher also had studied
with Mrs. Brown.

Take a moment now to record your personal response to the essay.
When you have finished, your instructor will suggest ways for class
members to share their impressions. You may be surprised by some of
the responses your classmates have, but you will discover how many
different impressions a single piece of writing can suggest.

By discussing the essay in class or by reading individual responses
out loud, you and your classmates probably arrived at general agreement about the author's main reason for writing the essay. You might
want to consider your classmates' ideas in evaluating your own response to the essay, but don't feel you have to agree with them when
you develop your response into a full-length paper. Your response to
the essay may have little to do with the author's apparent purpose. You
may focus on some other idea instead. But if the essay helped to stimulate your ideas, then it served as an inspiration for finding a writing
topic of your own. In other words, many things can help you find and
develop your topic: the essay itself, your initial response, other people's
responses, and discussion of all these ideas in class.

Now let's look at four students' responses to "Mary and Mrs.
Brown" and how one student developed his response into a complete
essay.

SAMPLE RESPONSES to "Mary and Mrs. Brown"

Responder 1: Michael ————————————————

This was one of those phony stories about a
dedicated teacher who helps a troubled child to adjust
to school and become a better person at the same time. I
can tell it's phony because I never had any teachers
like Mrs. Brown. Most of the teachers I had couldn't
wait to get to the parking lot when the last bell rang.
Who does this writer think she can fool? Maybe Mrs.
Brown is meant to be an example of what every teacher
should be, but there are no Mrs. Browns in the real
world.

Responder 2: Carol ————————————————

At first I liked Mrs. Brown fine, but as the story
moved ahead I saw that she was going much too far for a
teacher. By going too far, I mean that she should not
have bought the girl a sweater. The valentine was a bit
too much, too. Yes, Mary was an unhappy girl, and the
teacher was smart to notice that. But then she should
have sent Mary to a counselor, and they would have
talked to Mary's mother. It seems to me that Mrs. Brown
was trying to be a good mother for Mary, and that is not a
good idea. I also wonder what the other kids thought
when they saw what was happening. Some teachers spend

too much time worrying about the losers. They need to
spend more time with the normal students who may need a
little extra help, too.

Responder 3: Stanley

My younger sister is just like Mary. She is driving
my parents crazy because they don't know what to do
about her. She is always getting into trouble and she is
doing badly in school. She hangs out with a bad crowd and
listens to them rather than to our parents or to my older
sister and me. She really has me worried because I can't
see how she is going to avoid getting into worse trouble
if she keeps this up much longer.

Responder 4: Elissa

Mrs. Brown was one of those rare, special teachers
who just seems to know what a student needs to pull
himself or herself together. How Mrs. Brown helped Mary
can't really be taught—the teacher either has a special
insight with children's problems or she hasn't. It's
something like being a great artist—you're either born
with outstanding talent or you're not. However, we can't
expect all teachers to be great teachers, just as we
can't expect all artists to be great artists or all
doctors to be great doctors. There are differences among
great teachers, just as there are differences among
great artists. Mrs. Brown was outstanding in helping the

```
students to overcome personal problems, but other

teachers are skilled in other ways--the way they can get

students to understand difficult material, for

instance. As a mother, I give thanks that there are

teachers like Mrs. Brown, teachers who realize the

infinite value of every student.
```

From First Response to Complete Essay

We asked the four students to tell us how they moved from their first responses to the topics they eventually developed into an essay. No doubt their mental processes were more complicated than they were able to recall, but the explanations they offered do give us insights into how the reading-responding approach works. First, though, we promised to look closely at how one of these students (Michael) modified his first response as a result of ideas that came out during class discussion of the essay. Then we'll see how Michael's classmates responded to the first draft of his paper and how their criticism led him to edit and polish his final essay. Look again at Michael's response and notice that, throughout the drafting and revising process, it remains his chief motive for writing.

Michael's first response to the essay was quite negative. In fact, he called it "phony" and characterized Mrs. Brown as a fictitious example of an ideal teacher. When Michael sat down to write his paper, he intended to prove that the author had invented her picture of Mrs. Brown, who, for Michael, was clearly too good to be true. Then he remembered the class discussion, in which a number of students had mentioned teachers from their past who were highly conscientious. Michael realized that his own experience might have been somewhat limited and that teachers like Mrs. Brown might really exist. He reconsidered his plan to expose the phoniness he found in the essay. But he still was not ready to give up his negative response. It made him angry to think about all the less-than-ideal teachers he had encountered in his school years, and so he decided to write a paper about them—teachers who did *not* try to understand, much less to help, their students. Michael began by thinking of all the teachers he had known who "didn't care." Here is the first draft of his paper.

Teachers Who Didn't Care

I've had many teachers in my life who just didn't care about students. Sure, I've had some good teachers, too, but they were definitely in the minority. Most of the teachers I've had couldn't have cared less about helping me to learn and do well in school.

Take my high school geometry teacher for example. His name was Mr. D. That guy hated students—and especially me. I don't know why Mr. D. ever became a teacher. Can you imagine someone who can't stand the sight of blood wanting to become a doctor? Well, that's how it was with Mr. D. Why did he become a teacher if he couldn't stand the sight of students?

Mr. D. started the term by saying that he didn't expect more than half of us to pass the course. Great! There were about twenty-five of us in the class, so you can imagine how we felt. We had a 50-50 chance of passing, and with my track record in math, the odds were even longer.

Right after the first test, on which I scored a big fat 45, I knew I was in trouble. After he handed back the papers, I asked Mr. D. if he was going over the test in class so we could find out where we went wrong. He gave me a look that could have melted a stone statue. Then he said that he didn't want to waste time going over what he had already taught. He told me to study the textbook and help myself. Wonderful! That textbook might have been written in Japanese for all the sense I could make of it. When I told Mr. D that I couldn't understand the text, he replied that my test score was proof enough of that. He said it right in front of the whole class, just to embarrass me, I'm sure.

My father came to school and asked Mr. D if he would give me some extra help. Mr. D was as smooth as cream when he spoke to my father. Of course he would help. He was only too happy to put in extra time with students who needed it. Big deal! His idea of "extra time" consisted of five minutes going over a homework assignment with me. He went through the problems so fast that I couldn't follow a thing he said. Then he told me that he was on his break period and had other, more important things to do.

Naturally, I failed the course and had to take geometry in summer school in order to graduate on time. The summer school teacher was much better at explaining how to solve the problems. And she didn't mind staying after class to give me some extra help with the toughest problems. With her help and some tutoring from my friend Bob, I managed to squeeze out a passing grade.

I also had an English teacher in high school who thought everyone had to write like Shakespeare before they could pass her course. She made me rewrite my first paper five times before she finally broke down and gave it a passing grade. In fact, I had to rewrite each of my essays at least twice in order to meet her so-called standards. She didn't care that she was ruining my weekends and making me a nervous wreck. I really earned the C+ she gave me for the course.

My French teacher was another slave driver. I was

pretty good at reading and writing French, but that
wasn't good enough for Mrs. L. I also had to speak French
with a perfect Paris accent. Whenever I was called on to
recite, Mrs. L made me repeat the words over and over
until she was satisfied that I sounded "somewhat
French." She didn't care how much she made me sweat.
Some teachers have no mercy.

So, as you can see, I've had my share of teachers who
didn't care about their students. If you ask me, most
teachers don't care.

Peer Responses: Constructive Criticism

Michael's instructor asked him if he would mind being the first student to have his essay duplicated and distributed to the class for discussion. The instructor explained that learning how to offer and receive constructive criticism would be a major feature of the semester's work. She emphasized that peer responses can be very helpful in learning what is effective or ineffective in the first draft of a paper. Such feedback, the instructor continued, helps students to find out how well they communicate with each other in writing. Michael did not have to agree with his classmates' comments—whether negative or positive—but the instructor advised him to consider peer responses carefully before revising his draft into the final paper.

Michael agreed to share the first draft with his classmates, realizing that, although peer responses might have an unpleasant side, the feedback would motivate him to improve his writing. Besides, he liked the idea of discovering what his classmates found interesting. By reading each other's essays, everyone would get to know each other better, and the class would be more personal as well as more productive.

A Sample of Peer Responses

The instructor distributed copies of Michael's first draft to the class, and this is what some of his peers had to say.

Instructor: Now that we've all read Michael's paper, why don't we start discussing it by offering our first impressions. Let's not be too analytical right off the bat. Instead, we'll just express how the paper struck us immediately after we read it, and maybe offer a brief explanation for why we felt as we did. Jerry, do you want to begin?

Jerry: I liked it a lot.

Instructor: Okay, by "like" I guess you mean that there was something about the paper that made you feel a certain way?

Jerry: Right. I liked the way Michael told the truth about teachers. I felt he was saying things I've wanted to say for a long time.

Instructor: For instance?

Jerry: How most teachers don't really care about students.

Peggy: I didn't get that from the essay. I think that Michael wasn't very . . . well, fair in his opinion about teachers.

Michael: Fair? What does "fair" have to do with it! I wanted to tell exactly how I felt.

Susan: But you were fair, too. You told us that you had your problems with some subjects in high school.

Michael: That's right. I wasn't trying to pretend I was a perfect student. In fact, I needed a lot of help. But when I asked for help, where were the Mrs. Browns? They weren't in my school, that's for sure.

Carlos: I like the way Michael wrote his ideas. I mean, you could tell he was mad, but he also showed a sense of humor.

Instructor: For instance?

Carlos: Like when he said he didn't know why Mr. D wanted to be a teacher, because it was like someone who couldn't stand the sight of blood wanting to become a doctor. I liked that part.

Stanley: I agree that Michael has a sarcastic sense of humor, but I want to go back to what Peggy said about fairness. I could see where the math teacher didn't care, but the other teachers Michael mentioned aren't in the same category.

Alan: I was thinking about that, too. The English teacher was very strict about what she wanted, but she cared. She made Michael work on his writing. I don't mind a teacher who's strict, as long as she's trying to help me learn.

Bettina: And the same goes for the French teacher, I think.

Instructor: So, what are we saying?

Peggy: That maybe Michael shouldn't mix up strict teachers with those who don't care.

Connie: Also, he said the summer school teacher was great. So how does that fit in with not caring? The title of the paper is "Teachers Who Didn't Care." But that's not what the whole essay is about. Shouldn't all the teachers Michael mentions be ones who didn't care?

Jerry: Yeah. That's right. All the teachers should be examples of bad teachers, not just Mr. D.

Instructor: Michael?

Michael: Well, they were examples . . . in a way . . . but . . . wait. Just let me think about this a minute.

Carol: Can I say something, please?

Instructor: You certainly may.

Carol: We're talking about Michael's paper as if we know better than he does what he wanted to say. That's what bothers me about English classes. "Why did the writer say this? Why did the writer say that?" Michael knows what he wanted to say, so what's the difference what we think? He doesn't need us to tell him how to write his paper.

Instructor: How about that, Michael? Do you feel that some of us are confusing our own ideas with those you have written?

Michael: Sometimes I feel the way Carol just said. But I have to admit that there's a difference between what I thought I said and what my paper actually says. Does that make any sense?

Instructor: I think so.

Michael: I mean, when I write something, I know what I want to say. But I can see that people get confused if you mix up ideas and things in a paper.

Lenny: It's a good paper. It's just that some of your examples don't fit in the way you thought they would.

Michael: Yeah, I see that now. I went overboard because I still get angry whenever I think of Mr. D. I didn't think enough about what I was writing. Maybe I should forget the whole thing and begin all over again.

Stanley: I don't think so. A lot of this paper is good. Maybe you should stick to writing just about Mr. D. You know, build up that part a little more. Then the essay will be better organized.

Instructor: How does Stanley's advice strike you, Michael?

Michael: I like it. There are a few more things I wouldn't mind saying about Mr. D.

Connie: I'm not sure Michael has to limit himself to writing about Mr. D. Couldn't he use the summer school teacher as an example of a teacher who did care? Then he could compare a good teacher with Mr. D, and we'd get a better idea of just how bad Mr. D was.

    Michael: That makes sense, too. So what should I do, Professor?

    Instructor: You're the writer. Think about these suggestions, and decide which approach you want to take when you revise your first draft. Does anyone have anything else to offer?

    Susan: Mostly, I like the way Michael wrote, but in a few places he used some words that just don't sound right.

    Instructor: For instance?

    Susan: He used "guy" when he talked about the math teacher, which I don't think is right. It's too slangy for an essay like this. And he said the French teacher was a "slave driver" who made him "sweat." Those words just don't sound right to me.

    Tony: I agree that "guy" doesn't belong in this paper. But the other words sound all right. What's wrong with them?

    Susan: "Perspire" is a better word than "sweat," and "slave driver" is a cliché.

    Tony: Oh, come on! Nobody would say a teacher "made me perspire"! Teachers make you *sweat*, man!

This discussion of Michael's first draft continued a bit longer, but you've probably read enough to understand the benefits of peer responses. Notice that Michael's classmates brought up a lot of ideas that he should consider in revising his draft. Besides learning how his peers felt about his ideas and how he communicated them, Michael got feedback about how the essay could be organized better, and he also got suggestions about the words he used.

Imagine yourself as one of Michael's classmates. What comments would you make about his first draft? Are your suggestions as constructive as those offered by Michael's peers? Which comments do you think were most helpful? Which were least helpful?

Now let's see how Michael reacted to peer responses. The second draft of his paper follows.

A Teacher Who Didn't Care

I've had many teachers in my life. Most of them

tried to help me to learn, even though there were things

about them that I didn't like. Some were so strict about

rules that they ran their classes as if the students

were soldiers. Others tried to be too friendly, and, as
a result, didn't get much done in class. Overall,
though, I feel these teachers cared about me as a person
and wanted me to learn. But I've also had some teachers
who didn't care whether I learned anything or not. The
worst of these was my high school geometry teacher, Mr.
D.

Mr. D started the term by saying that he didn't
expect more than half the class to pass the course. He
said this in such a cold, sarcastic way that nobody had
any doubt that he meant what he said. With my terrible
track record in math, I knew that I was all but doomed.
From that first day, I could tell that Mr. D hated
students. Can you imagine someone who couldn't stand the
sight of blood becoming a doctor? So why did Mr. D become
a teacher if he couldn't stand the sight of students?

After the first test, on which I scored an
embarrassing 45, I asked Mr. D if he would go over the
test in class so we could find out where we went wrong.
He gave me a look that could have melted a statue and
said that he didn't want to waste time going over what he
had already taught. He told me to study the textbook and
to figure things out for myself. Wonderful! That book
might have been written in Chinese for all the sense I
could make of it. When I told Mr. D I couldn't understand
the book's explanations, he replied that my test score
was proof enough of that. He said it right in front of
the whole class, just to embarrass me, I'm sure.

My father came to school and asked Mr. D to give me
some extra help. Mr. D, as smooth as cream, said that he

was only too happy to put in extra time with students who
needed it. I began to think that maybe he wasn't such a
hard-hearted person after all. But was I mistaken! Mr.
D's idea of "extra time" consisted of five minutes going
over a homework assignment with me. He went over the
problems so fast, I couldn't follow a thing he said.
Then he told me he was on his break period and had more
important things to do.

During one part of the term, I actually understood
the work more than I had up to that point. I studied
hard, because I thought if I could pass one of Mr. D's
tests, I might gain some confidence and maybe squeeze
out a passing grade for the course. The test wasn't
easy, but I felt that I had done enough problems
correctly to score at least the 65 that would pass.

When I got my paper back, there was a large 55 on it,
but I couldn't believe I had done that badly. I checked
my paper against the test of a friend who had gotten a
70. No matter how we figured, I had gotten enough right
answers to pass. So I showed my paper to Mr. D the next
day and asked if he had made a mistake. He told me there
was no mistake. He had deducted ten points because I
hadn't shown clearly enough how I had solved the
problems. And he wasn't interested in going over the
test with me, so I could show him that the figuring was
there, even if it was a little sloppy and hard to read.
After that I had no confidence at all. I couldn't pass
one of Mr. D's tests, even when I passed one.

Naturally I failed the course and had to take
geometry in summer school in order to graduate on time.

Luckily for me—and for the other fourteen students who failed Mr. D's course—Ms. L taught the geometry class that summer. She had a way of making math much easier to understand. She made up problems of her own that were much more interesting and helpful than the problems in the textbook. And best of all, she didn't mind staying after class to give extra help. Sometimes she became frustrated when I kept coming up with wrong answers to easy problems, but I could tell that she didn't think I was stupid. In fact, she told me I had a perfectly good mind but that geometry wasn't my best subject. What a difference from Mr. D, who went out of his way to make me feel like a hopeless case.

I passed geometry that summer, and so did about ninety percent of the class. It wasn't because Ms. L was an easy marker. Her exams were just as tough as Mr. D's. The difference was that I had actually learned something from Ms. L.

Mr. D was a teacher who didn't care about students. Luckily, Ms. L did care, so my term with Mr. D didn't permanently destroy my confidence. Still, I feel sorry for all the students who have teachers like Mr. D and never get the chance to regain their confidence from a teacher like Ms. L.

Considering the Second Draft

Michael's second draft shows that peer responses had definite effects on his thinking and writing. Consider the following questions and think about the decisions Michael made when he revised his paper.

- Which peer responses did Michael take seriously? To what extent did classmates' suggestions affect the organization of his paper?
- Which peer responses did Michael ignore or not take seriously? Do you agree with his decisions?
- Did all of Michael's changes and additions improve his first draft? Which changes, if any, do you think Michael should not have made?
- What advice would you give Michael if he asked you how he could improve the second draft of his paper?

Other Responses, Other Essays

Earlier in the chapter we showed four responses to the essay "Mary and Mrs. Brown." We then concentrated on Michael's response to show how he benefited from the reading-responding process. Let's return now to those other students. As we will see, Responders 2 and 3, Carol and Stanley, also developed their initial ideas through peer responses to arrive at their essays. But Responder 4, Elissa, switched her topic entirely and ended up focusing on one of her classmate's responses, which she felt took a wrongheaded approach to students like Mary.

Before each of the following essays is a brief description of how the writer arrived at his or her final topic. These essays, along with Michael's, show the variety of responses and topics that can be triggered by a single piece of writing. Each essay reflects the unique response of its writer. Before reading the essays, however, look back at the three students' initial responses to "Mary and Mrs. Brown."

Responder 2: Carol

Most of Carol's classmates agreed with her criticism of Mrs. Brown for buying Mary gifts. They felt that a teacher shouldn't buy things for a student, even if the gifts did somehow help a maladjusted student to feel better about herself. The consensus was that such a practice could get out of hand and could encourage other students to misbehave, hoping to receive a "bribe" from the teacher for good behavior. The class did not agree, however, about how much time and effort a teacher should spend on troubled students. About half the class thought that a good teacher would give extra attention to students whose personal problems interfered with their schoolwork. But there was also strong support for the idea that teachers should be concerned primarily with helping students to understand subject matter, and that they should not see themselves as psychological counselors.

Carol felt uneasy as she read about Mrs. Brown's special acts of kindness toward Mary. She wondered whether the other students were being neglected. The essay made her realize that she has never liked the way our society seems to care more about troublemakers than about the majority who get along nicely and follow the accepted standards of behavior. And as for students who experience difficulty learning their subjects, Carol believed that all of them—not just those who are troubled—should receive the teacher's attention. As a result of peer responses and further thinking, Carol decided to write about the need for teachers to ignore the losers and concentrate on the average and better students. Her first draft follows.

Misplaced Kindness

At first the story of how Mrs. Brown helped Mary made me feel good because I enjoy reading about kind people. But then I began to think about the other students in Mrs. Brown's class who also needed help. Maybe they were not as needy as Mary, but they could have used some extra attention to make them good students instead of just average ones. When a teacher spends too much time and energy on the losers, the rest of the students have to improve all by themselves. Most of them cannot do it alone, and so that means Mrs. Brown was not a good example of a perfect teacher.

Many of the students in my classes were like Mary in some way or another, and most of the teachers, especially in grade school, gave time to these "difficult" students. That meant that the rest of us had to sit around very bored, or else we fooled around, while those teachers played Mommy to misbehaving children or those who did not really care about school.

I resented the fact that these teachers did not help me to do better in math and science, my worst enemies.

The writer wants us to believe that Mrs. Brown's efforts paid off in a big way for Mary, but I would not bet any money on how well Mary ever did as a result of all that love and TLC. Some of the students in my classes who received extra attention are now unable to hold a job. What good did that special treatment do them? Furthermore, most of those losers never really wanted the extra help; they just did not dare refuse it. But the worst part of all this is that some of my friends who barely managed to pass are now running into trouble as they try to handle college work. If that extra help had gone to them, they would have made good use of it and would not be struggling to survive now.

I think that the article was meant to make teachers feel guilty if they are not giving all of themselves to their students, especially those at the bottom. This writer thinks she knows what is best, but she really does not understand the students. Doesn't she realize that most dropouts just plain do not like school? All they want to do is hang out. They actually resent teachers meddling in their personal lives. My advice to the teachers of the world is to concentrate on those who can really use their help. Let the losers stay lost.

Responder 3: Stanley

In a small-group discussion with classmates, Stanley said that he had not been able to concentrate on the essay very well because he was worried about his sister's behavior. He realized his response may have seemed a little strange because it grew out of his personal distress rather than what the writer of "Mary and Mrs. Brown" was saying. He could not help identifying his sister with Mary, even though his sister was older than Mary and her problems seemed more severe. The group encouraged Stanley to write about his sister, since that was how he responded to the essay.

Stanley was almost convinced, but he thought he should check this idea with his instructor because he wasn't sure it was a proper topic. Stanley's instructor understood why he had responded to the essay as he did, and she added that people are sometimes able to relieve tension and anxiety by writing about their feelings. She encouraged Stanley to develop his response into a paper about his sister's behavior, even though the topic did not follow directly from the essay. The important thing for all writers, she said, is to discover a topic that truly means something to them. Stanley then wrote the following paper.

A Young Woman in Big Trouble

My own adolescence had its ups and downs, but for the most part I enjoyed growing up. Maybe things went well for me because I moved ahead at a normal pace, and I got along pretty well with my parents most of the time. On the other hand, my fourteen-year-old sister, Joann, seems to be having a very rough time. She hardly speaks to Mom and Dad, and she has fallen in with a wild bunch who are always getting into trouble of one kind or another. I wish some understanding person could see Joann's need for help and find some way to reach out to her. I believe Joann's tough attitude is just her way of keeping her personal pain hidden from the world. Somebody outside our family must get through to her before she wrecks her life.

Joann's problem goes back a long way. She came along when I was seven and my older sister Clare was nine. Mother had gone back to her job as a pediatric nurse and

did not want to return to the role of housewife/mother.
So babysitters were hired to care for Joann until she
was old enough to go to kindergarten. None of them
stayed very long. When I think back about Joann as a
small child, I see a sour-faced brat, whose tears and
shouts seemed fake about half the time.

School solved the babysitting problem because
Clare and I could be assigned that job when we came home
from school. I resented having to look after Joann, and
I probably took my frustration out on her some of the
time. Then she hit sixth grade, and everything changed.

When Joann, who wins the prize for good looks in our
family, turned twelve, she became popular in school for
the first time. Not with the teachers--she has never
done well on report cards, especially in "attitude"--
but with those girls who dress like Madonna and act like
they are eighteen. When Mother saw Joann's rapid
transformation, she began criticizing her behavior,
instead of just complaining as we had all been doing for
years. Clare and I felt our parents were being a bit hard
on Joann, but we were not worried then because we had
fought with them about those things ourselves.

Recently, it became clear to us that the group of
girls Joann hangs out with are even more rebellious than
we had thought. They spend their afternoons and weekends
with guys who are much older and wilder than is good for
someone Joann's age. When Clare and I try to talk to
Joann about the situation, she will not listen. She
tells us to mind our own business.

Since I cannot see Joann responding to any of us, I

desperately hope that someone she can respect will come

along and take note of her troubled condition. She needs

a true friend, and soon!

Responder 4: Elissa

When Elissa heard some of her classmates criticize Mrs. Brown for "wasting the other students' time on a loser like Mary," she wanted to rise to the teacher's defense. Having raised a family before returning to college, Elissa believed she had learned something about life, and in her view the idea of labeling people as "losers" could have grave effects on those persons' lives. After the class had discussed each other's responses, Elissa forgot how strongly she felt about this issue, and she proceeded to write an essay that supported the general idea that teachers like Mrs. Brown are rare and valuable. However, she found it difficult to say something distinctly different from what she had read. Even though she added a couple of examples from her own earlier days in school, the essay as a whole didn't seem to carry much punch. She felt it sounded like an echo of "Mary and Mrs. Brown."

When the instructor asked one morning whether anyone was having trouble writing the essay, Elissa raised her hand and described her predicament. Remembering that Elissa had rather forcefully defended the helping of so-called losers, the instructor asked Elissa if she still felt as strongly about that issue. Reminded of her reaction to the other student's response, Elissa asked whether she could still switch topics. The instructor assured her that the purpose of sharing responses was to allow each student to find the best possible topic, and Elissa decided to write about her strongest feelings. As you will see, her essay came out very nicely.

A Response to the Writer Who Would Abandon "Losers"

When we were asked to present our responses to "Mary

and Mrs. Brown," I expected the usual boring class

discussion. But I was amazed to find that some people

felt Mrs. Brown was not an outstanding teacher. I was

especially surprised to hear some people refer to

students with problems as "losers." When I was in high

school, I had trouble in several subjects, and if some

teachers hadn't gone out of their way for this "loser,"
I would not be here today.

The word "loser" is very offensive, for it says the
speaker is a "winner." The winner/loser view of life
causes many of the problems in our world today. You're
not a winner unless you own a huge house, drive
expensive cars, have all the latest video and audio
systems, spend vacations in faraway places, etc. The
winners all use the right soap, drink the right beer,
wear the "in" jeans. Anyone else is a nerd and a loser.
Winning girls don't even notice losing boys, and vice
versa. Sports are fun only if you win; business is full
of cheaters competing to be winners.

This attitude sees most people as losers. And that
means a lot of average people working at everyday jobs,
enjoying simple pleasures, are losers who are obviously
missing something valuable in their lives. This leaves a
lot of people feeling lousy while they are envying the
winners. Advertising encourages this attitude in its
efforts to sell things that promise to make us feel like
winners. All this is so wrong. There is no winning in
life, only moments in happiness. I'd rather live a happy
life, enjoying my relationships with people who mean
something to me because they love me and I love them.

School is where this win/lose attitude starts.
There, knowing fewer than 65 answers to 100 questions is
considered losing. No one asks what difference it makes
whether you know all that information. Most of it is
soon forgotten anyway. Some people learn more easily
than others, generally because they have a special

talent (English, math) or because they really like a
subject (history, science). That's fine, but the others
shouldn't be thought of as losers. Soon they began to
feel like losers, and this negative feeling can carry
over to the rest of their lives, unless they have a
talent for playing sports or for being popular, which
allows them to win a big game or a beautiful girlfriend
or boyfriend.

A sensitive teacher like Mrs. Brown knows how
important it is to keep children from becoming "losers."
She tried to help a troubled student feel she was worth
something to someone. Mary may have trouble holding a
job after she graduates (and she may not graduate
without help from some other Mrs. Browns). But that's
not a sign of losing. Who knows where she may end up
years later? She may raise a happy family and truly
enjoy the simple parts of life—weddings, family
picnics, watching TV with family and friends, walking
through a park, reading, cooking delicious meals,
helping a neighbor out of trouble, feeling close to her
husband. If she believes she is a loser, maybe she won't
be able to enjoy these experiences, because she'll be
reminded by TV and all those would-be winners that the
simple joys are not good enough.

A REVIEW OF THE PROCESS
(How *You* Should Use This Book)

Now that you have been through the reading-responding process that forms the basis of this book, let's review the steps and activities that make up the process. The following suggestions about reading and responding will help you prepare to write your essay.

1. Start by reading the assignment and recording your strongest first impressions. Don't analyze the essay or story during this first reading. Instead, let your thoughts run free. At this point you are less interested in what the author had in mind than you are in what comes to *your* mind as you read.

2. Depending on your instructor's guidance, share your impressions and responses through class discussion, by exchanging your ideas with one or more classmates, or by working in small groups. Even friends and roommates who aren't in this class can be helpful during this stage. By trying out your ideas on others, you will think about the essay or story in greater detail and will gain insights into why you responded as you did.

3. When you have a fairly clear idea of what you want to write about, decide upon a topic and begin to write. Remember that the topic you first select may not be the one that you finally write about. Michael, for example, changed the title of his essay because of peer responses to his first draft. In any case, the topic you choose at this point will help you to organize your ideas as you begin to write your first draft.

4. When you have completed your first draft, put it aside for a day or two. This "break" from your work will allow you to reread your draft with the fresh eyes of a reader coming to your words for the first time. When you do reread the draft, you probably will note places where it could be improved through revision. Any time you have to pause or reread a passage in order to remember what you had in mind, you know you need to revise. After all, if you, the writer, have difficulty following the flow of the ideas, your readers are certain to have problems. This is your chance to edit any confusing or awkward passages. Now copy your revised first draft neatly and submit it for peer responses to see how well you have expressed your ideas.

5. Peer responses may be gathered through class discussion of

your first draft, such as the discussion of Michael's paper. But feedback and constructive criticism can also take place in a small, informal group or in conversations with anyone whose opinions you value. The important point is that you share your first draft and get some sort of peer response, for nothing can replace the insights you will gain from other people's reactions to your writing.

6. After you have discussed your paper with peers, the next step is to decide which of their suggestions and criticism you want to apply in revising the paper. The ability to select suggestions that will strengthen your essays is a vital part of writing, and your ability to do so will improve with each assignment. Be prepared for criticism, and ask yourself *why* your peers responded as they did to your first draft. Even a remark that you consider foolish or insulting may contain a germ of truth—if you listen to it with an open mind.

7. Now you are ready to revise your first draft to reflect those peer responses that you find valuable. Focus especially on suggestions about the organization and wording of your ideas. Did every example you offered contribute to the overall point you wanted to make, or did some readers wonder why you included a particular detail? Did anyone object to your language? Was anyone confused by a point that seemed clear to you? Did your peers find the essay satisfying and complete, or did they feel it just sort of wandered off? Maybe you need to strengthen the conclusion of your paper so that readers will put it down knowing exactly what you meant.

Professional writers know that the process of editing never stops, for the reactions of readers always lead them to see new ideas and ways of saying things. No doubt your second draft also could be improved by seeking further feedback and revising the paper one more time. At some point, however, the writer decides to publish the paper and move on to other things. In this book, too, we encourage you to end the reading-responding process when you have completed your second draft. Move on to the next reading, which will offer a new opportunity to express yourself.

PART ONE

Responding to People

The readings in Part One express writers' ideas and feelings about themselves and about other people. Such essays are likely to stimulate your own ideas and feelings about people you know or have known. You may want to write about someone important in your life, or you may be moved to express something about yourself. As you learned in the Introduction, each reader responds to a piece of writing in unique, unpredictable ways. The best way to discover what impact one of these readings has on you is to record your strongest response to it as soon as you finish reading. Then follow the process illustrated in the Introduction to develop an essay of your own. First, share your response with your classmates, and use their comments to adjust and expand the ideas you plan to write about. Then share your first draft with your peers, and consider their constructive criticism carefully when you revise the draft into your finished essay.

The first four essays in Part One are followed by sample responses, like those in the Introduction, to help you assess your own ideas. In addition, we have provided comments and questions to guide you in considering the sample responses and how they can be developed into complete essays. You should raise similar questions about your own responses and those of your classmates.

Without Emotion

G. GORDON LIDDY

Squirrel hunting was a popular sport in West Caldwell in the 1940s. I loaded my homemade rifle, cocked the spring, and waited on the steps of the porch. A squirrel was in the top of the pear tree. I raised the rifle. The movement startled the squirrel and he jumped to the oak tree and froze as I stepped off the porch. I sighted along the side of the barrel, aimed for the squirrel's head, and fired.

I missed the squirrel's head and gut-shot him. Bravely, he clung to the tree as long as he could, then started to come down, clutching piteously at branches as he fell, wounded mortally.

I didn't know it, but the shot alerted my mother. She watched the furry creature's descent until it fell to the ground and I shot it again, this time through the head at point-blank range, to put it out of its suffering, then cut off its tail to tie to the handlebars of my bicycle as an ornament.

When I came into the house my mother told me reproachfully that she had seen from the kitchen window the suffering I had caused. I went off and wept. The dying squirrel haunted me. I kept seeing it fall, clutching and clawing from what must have been a terribly painful wound. I was furious with myself—not because I'd caused the pain, though I regretted that, but because I hadn't been able to kill without emotion. How could I expect to be a soldier in the war? I had to do something to free myself from this disabling emotionalism.

I cast about for an idea and found it across the street. Bill Jacobus's father, to help combat the wartime food shortage and to supplement rationing, had built a chicken coop in his backyard. He and his son used to butcher the chickens, then drain, scald, pluck, and clean them for sale.

I asked young Bill if I could help kill the chickens. He was glad to have the help. He showed me how to grasp the bird in such a way as to have control of both wings and feet, lay its neck on an upended stump, and then decapitate it with one chop of an ax held in the other hand. Bill explained that the shock made the corpse convulse and, if I let go, the body would run about, wings flapping, and bruise the meat. I'd need to control the corpse until the shock wore off and the limp body could be hung up by the feet to drain the remaining blood. I should wear my old clothes.

Using the ax tentatively rather than making a bold stroke, I made a   7
mess of my first chicken kill; it took me a number of chops to get the head off. The bird slipped out of my grasp and half flew, half jumped about, blood spurting from its neck all over me and everything else in range. Bill was good about it and gave me another chance.

I got better at it, and over a period of time I killed and killed and   8
killed, getting less and less bloody, swifter and swifter, surer with my ax stroke until, finally, I could kill efficiently and without emotion or thought. I was satisfied: when it came my turn to go to war, I would be ready. I could kill as I could run—like a machine.

SAMPLE RESPONSES to "Without Emotion"

Responder 1: Maria ————————————————————

Liddy has the kind of mentality that keeps the human race going from one war to another throughout all of history. It's people like Liddy who can't wait for the first gun to be fired so they can kill people without going to prison. In fact he wants to kill enough people that he will be awarded a medal saying he's a hero. We must keep our eyes on someone like Liddy to make sure he doesn't get any power if we want to keep the earth from being destroyed in a nuclear war. Squirrels and chickens are just a warmup for a guy who loves war. What he would really like to do is to drop a few H–bombs on small countries that couldn't retaliate. Even if it led to World War III and everybody, including him, was killed, that wouldn't bother a guy like Liddy who's in love with war and death. This character scares the hell out of me.

Responder 2: Atkins ——————————————————

It takes great discipline and training to make good
soldiers. Liddy wanted to be prepared for combat just in
case his service was needed to defend our country. His
childhood happened during the war with Germany and Japan
when people believed America was right and were willing
to die for democracy. Today many people would say Liddy
is crazy because they don't believe in America any more.
They want to live here, but they don't want to risk their
skin defending the USA. A lot of my friends would leave
the country rather than fight in a war. That's terrific!
Who do they think will stop the enemy from marching into
their houses and killing and raping their families? The
world was lucky these guys weren't around when Hitler
and Tojo were trying to conquer the world.

Responder 3: Sydney ——————————————————

Sick! Sick! Sick! Sick! Sick! Sick!

Responder 4: Caroline ——————————————————

I despise persons who think animals were put on
earth to be tortured and killed for human pleasure.
Animals are living things and have feelings just like
people. They also feel pain and pleasure. Their lives
are valuable to them, and to God, even if brave men like
Gordon Liddy don't place any value on them. Brave little

Gordon Liddy thought he had the right to decide when animals should die if he felt like having some target practice. Recently, I saw a television picture of baby seals being mercilessly clubbed to death in Canada so that rich women could wear their beautiful fur. That was the most horrible scene I've seen in years. If I were president I'd have those men shot. I know I will never wear a fur coat or anything else made from the skins of innocent animals.

Responder 5: Brad

G. Gordon Liddy was convicted of breaking into Democratic party headquarters during the Watergate scandal which forced Richard Nixon to abdicate. Now this convicted felon writes his memoirs and some immoral publishing company sells them for millions. This disgraceful transaction reveals the profound depths which our once great nation has fallen into. The heads of today's Americans have more holes than Swiss cheese. They read a crook's confessions as if it was another inane soap opera; worse yet, they spend good money on such rubbish. Liddy's rich; Nixon's rich; any criminal can become wealthy if his crime makes the TV news. Corrupt people become heroes in our decadent society. How can we expect America to regain its rightful place as world leader as long as these disgusting people's lives are presented as models for children to look up to and envy.

CONSIDERING THE RESPONSES

Response 1: Maria

Maria sees Liddy as an example of the kind of people she intensely dislikes and even fears. Notice two phrases that Maria used which reveal the "example" approach: "It's people like Liddy . . ." and "We must keep our eyes on someone like Liddy. . ." Do you think Maria could use examples to expand this response into an essay that develops her ideas about people like Liddy? Can you think of any problems she might have in using examples to support her opinion? Would Liddy still be the focus of her essay, or would he appear in a minor role?

Response 2: Atkins

Atkins admired Liddy's determination to be ready for war if America ever needed him. He pointed out the reasons for Liddy's patriotism and contrasted Liddy's attitudes with those of his friends and most young Americans today. What other ideas do you see in this response to the Liddy piece? Do you believe that patriotism or the lack of it is the main idea Atkins should explore? Why or why not?

Response 3: Sydney

Although Sydney's response is unusually brief, it does indicate a strong emotional reaction to the reading. What to you think Sydney felt that caused him to respond by writing the same word six times? What must Sydney do before he can develop his response into an essay?

Response 4: Caroline

Caroline's response shows less concern with Liddy than with an issue which the reading raised in her mind. What do you think is the issue Caroline is concerned about? Do you think she has tied that issue closely enough to Liddy's piece in her response? Why or why not? How would *you* tie Liddy's comments to the issue on Caroline's mind?

Response 5: Brad ⎯⎯⎯⎯⎯⎯⎯⎯⎯⎯⎯⎯⎯⎯⎯⎯⎯⎯

Brad, like Maria, sees Liddy as an example of a kind of person he dislikes. What do you think is the basis for Brad's negative reaction to Liddy? Do you see any way that Brad can express his deep concerns and still focus on Liddy? What approach do you think Brad should take?

Good News

ROBERT FULGHUM

How about some good news for a change? Something to con- 1
sider when you are in a people-are-no-damn-good mood?

Here's a phrase we hear a lot: "You can't trust anybody anymore." 2
Doctors and politicians and merchants and salesmen. They're all out to
rip you off, right?

It ain't necessarily so. 3

Man named Steven Brill tested the theory. In New York City, with 4
taxicab drivers. Brill posed as a well-to-do foreigner with little knowledge of English. He got into several dozen taxis around New York City
to see how many drivers would cheat him. His friends predicted in
advance that most would take advantage of him in some way.

One driver out of thirty-seven cheated him. The rest took him di- 5
rectly to his destination and charged him correctly. Several refused to
take him when his destination was only a block or two away, even getting out of their cabs to show him how close he already was. The greatest irony of all was that several drivers warned him that New York City
was full of crooks and to be careful.

You will continue to read stories of crookedness and corruption— 6
of policemen who lie and steal, doctors who reap where they do not
sew, politicians on the take. Don't be misled. They are news because
they are the exceptions. The evidence suggests that you can trust a lot
more people than you think. The evidence suggests that a lot of people
believe that. A recent survey by Gallup indicates that 70 percent of the
people believe that most people can be trusted most of the time.

Who says people are no damn good? What kind of talk is that? 7

SAMPLE RESPONSES to "Good News"

Responder 1: Franklin ————————————

I don't know about taxicab drivers in New York City, but I do know what I read in the newspaper a couple of weeks ago. It was a story that also concerned a test of people's honesty.

An inspector from a consumer protection agency in one of our larger cities drove a car to twenty different auto repair shops. A consumer agency mechanic had doctored the car so that it had a minor problem that should have cost about forty dollars to fix. But only three of the repair stations offered to fix the car for under fifty dollars. The owners of all the other stations claimed that the car had a major problem that would require extensive repairs. Their estimates ranged from 200 to 600 dollars. This test doesn't make people look as honest as the taxicab driver test that Fulghum writes about. So where do we stand in relation to honesty?

Responder 2: Maxine ————————————

I think that people who go through life thinking that everybody is out to cheat them lead miserable lives. These people spend all their time figuring out

how this person or that person is trying to screw them
out of something.

Me, I take the opposite approach. I just assume that
most people are honest. I know that sounds naive, but I
think my approach is best. Sure, I've been cheated by
people a few times in my life. Mostly, though, people
have treated me honestly and fairly. I'd rather live
with the idea that most people are honest than to live
with the fear that at any moment somebody might steal
the socks off my feet.

Responder 3: Cal ─────────────────────────────

This author is probably a nice man who wants to
divide human beings into good people and bad people,
with the good people making up almost all of the
population. That's a comforting thought. But I don't
think it works that way. Nobody is absolutely honest or
absolutely dishonest. Probably everybody has something
about which he or she is dishonest. For example, many
students who wouldn't steal money or property don't
think twice about cheating on tests in school. Also,
many people who are good citizens 99 percent of the time
think nothing about cheating on their income taxes.

So what I'm saying is that it would be hard to find
people who are absolutely honest or people who are
absolutely dishonest. Almost all of us are dishonest
about some things if we look at ourselves closely.

Responder 4: Milo _____

I don't believe this writer's story about the cab
drivers--especially cab drivers in a big city like New
York. I'm sure he made up the story to make his readers
feel good. I've been in a lot of places all over the
world, and the one thing that's the same about all of
them is that people will try to rip you off if they think
they can get away with it. I should know--I've been
ripped off plenty in my time. Take my advice and don't
believe this writer. Anybody who believes that most
people are honest deserves to be taken advantage of.
Remember--I warned you.

CONSIDERING THE RESPONSES

Responder 1: Franklin _____

Franklin ended his response by writing: "So where do we stand in relation to honesty?" The class came to the general agreement that Franklin's question was a difficult one to answer, especially when the results of the two tests were compared. Assuming that the results of both tests are accurate, do you think Franklin could write an essay in which he tries to explain why the results of the tests differed so much? What are some of the questions Franklin might raise about the way the tests were carried out? Does Franklin have to "solve" the honesty question in order to write an interesting essay?

Responder 2: Maxine _____

Maxine seems to agree with Fulghum's optimistic view of people's honesty, and quite a few students agreed that her trusting approach was the best way to go through life. After some discussion, which also included comments implying that Maxine was indeed naive, a student suggested that Maxine could write a lively essay in which she contrasts the advantages of her trusting approach to the disadvantages of an untrusting approach to people's honesty. Do you have any suggestions about how Maxine might plan such an essay? What would Maxine have to have clearly in mind before attempting an essay based upon contrasts?

Responder 3: Cal

Students saw several possibilities for essays arising from Cal's response. One suggestion was for Cal to write an essay in which he tries to explain why people who are generally honest in most ways go against their sense of honesty in certain situations. Do you think Cal should go into some depth in attempting to explain one case—such as students who resort to dishonesty only when worried about their performance on tests—or should he deal with a number of such possible cases? Students also suggested Cal could write a good paper by expanding on the idea in the last sentence of his response: "Almost all of us are dishonest about something if we look at ourselves closely." Would an essay based upon this idea call on Cal to investigate his own approach to honesty?

Responder 4: Milo

During class discussion, Milo conceded that his negative feelings toward the honesty of people had grown out of a number of bad experiences he'd had in different places throughout the world and that he was probably judging *all* people too harshly on the basis of these experiences. One student suggested that Milo might recount a number of his experiences in an essay, and by so doing, see if there were some sort of pattern in his being "ripped-off" so often. "Maybe you can advise us against dealing with certain kinds of people; or perhaps you can help us to know what kinds of situations to avoid," the student suggested. What do you think of this suggestion?

A Fling on the Track

BILL COSBY

During my last year of high school, I fell in love so hard with a 1
girl that it made my love for Sarah McKinney seem like a stupid infat-
uation with a teacher. Charlene Gibson was the Real Thing and she
would be Mrs. Charlene Cosby, serving me hot dogs and watching me
drive to the hoop and giving me the full-court press for the rest of my
life.

In tribute to our great love, I was moved to give Charlene some- 2
thing to wear. A Temple T-shirt didn't seem quite right and neither
did my Truman button. What Charlene needed was a piece of jewelry;
and I was able to find the perfect one, an elegant pin, in my mother's
dresser drawer.

Ten days after I made this grand presentation, Charlene dumped 3
me; but, sentimentalist that she was, she kept the pin. When I con-
fessed my dark deed to my mother, she didn't throw a brick at me, she
merely wanted to have the pin back, a request that I felt was not unreasonable since I had stolen it. Moreover, retrieving the pin was important to *me*, but for a romantic notion: I wanted to punish Charlene.
Paying back the person with whom you have recently been in love is
one of life's most precious moments.

"I want that pin back," I said to Charlene on the phone. 4

"I can't do that," she replied. 5

Why not?" 6

"You *lost* it?" 7

"That's what I just said." 8

"How could you *lose* it?" 9

"Easy. First I had it, then I didn't." 10

And so, I went to her house, where her mother said she wasn't 11
home. Nervously I told her mother why I needed the pin returned and
she understood without saying I had done anything wrong. Of course,
she didn't have the world's sharpest judgment because she still thought
I was a wonderful person. In fact, *all* the mothers of the girls who
rejected me thought I was a wonderful person; I would have made a
fine father to those girls.

"Mrs. Gibson," I said, "Charlene told me she lost the pin. I'm not   12
saying I don't believe her, but I don't."

"Just one minute, William," she said, and she turned and went up-   13
stairs. Moments later, she returned with the pin. And then I went
home and waited for the satisfaction of Charlene calling me to say:

How dare you go to my house and ask my mother for that pin!   14

But no call from her came.   15

Probably because she's ashamed of lying to me, I told myself; *but maybe*   16
because she truly likes me and wants to keep the pin for that reason.

I was convincing myself that Charlene wanted to have an elegant   17
token of me and that now I should call *her* to rekindle this wondrous
love-hate relationship, for Charlene and I had been meant for each
other: she was a liar and I was a thief. Two such people, who had been
so deeply in love, should have had a chance to keep torturing each
other. We once had kissed for almost three hours, inhaling each other
and talking about how many children we should have. True, she was
the kind of girl who might be having children by other men too, but
there was still a softness about her I liked, a softness that matched the
one in my head. We had been too close for our relationship to end with
her dumping me. We had to get back together so I could dump *her*.

SAMPLE RESPONSES to "A Fling on the Track"

Responder 1: Paul

I know what he means about women; they will lead a
guy into thinking they like him, and then, without any
reason, they drop him. I've learned not to let myself
become too attached, or at least I don't let my feelings
show. I would never consider giving a girl anything
valuable as a sign of my affection. She'd probably do
what this girl did, or worse.

I think that when a man shows he is really interested
in a woman, the game is over——she has won. All she is
doing is playing a game, and when a guy falls for her,

she adds his shrunken head to her collection. The good—
looking chicks are all like this, it seems. And some of
the homely ones like to try it, too. I've seen my sisters
do this to guys, and when they are alone at home, they
laugh and boast about their conquests. My advice is:
Stay cool till you're certain you've got the upper hand
with a woman. Then, if there is any dropping to be done,
you'll be the one doing it.

Responder 2: Cindy

Many young men have been victimized by girls like
the one Bill Cosby dated, and they come to believe that
all attractive women are equally dangerous. I have
witnessed similar situations myself, and I think I know
why the women behave this way. They are afraid of
entering a deep relationship. They are pleased when an
attractive man returns their interest, but they want the
relationship to remain relatively cool and easy going.
Receiving a major gift, like a piece of jewelry, could
cause considerable consternation in these women. Their
pleasure could be overcome by anxiety as to what they
are expected to do in return for the gift and the great
compliment that comes with it. So they end the
relationship abruptly because they don't want to have
to explain themselves.

The girl was wrong to keep the pin. I can't imagine
what confused thoughts were going through her head, but
I would not be so sure her intentions were sadistic.

Maybe she wanted to keep the pin as a beautiful sign of having been loved, and so she talked herself into believing that "a gift is a gift" and the giver has no right to ask for its return. That is not logical, but it's not evil either.

Responder 3: Margaret

I went through something like this once, too, only it happened with a boy who treated me like a slave once I let him know I thought he was wonderful. Matt did not stop seeing me, and I did not give him a present. But I did give him my heart, and that's when he began to treat me horribly. We'd go out with other couples, and he'd continually put me down, saying, "Of course, Maggie wouldn't understand this" and "Mag could never do that!" and "Only Maggie would believe such and such." Actually, he was rather nice when we were alone, but it wasn't long before his bad attitude took over completely. Yet I kept on hoping this was just a phase. I thought he was testing my love for him. Boy, was I ever kidding myself! I felt so foolish when he told me he was seeing another girl, one of my best friends! I warned her about him, but she probably thought she was much more attractive than me, and therefore, Matt would be true to her. At the end of the summer, she was telling everyone what a louse he was. Too many good-looking men and women get to thinking they are so superior that they can pick up and discard people the way rich women buy and throw away clothes.

CONSIDERING THE RESPONSES

Responder 1: Paul ————————————————

The class reacted to Paul's response either by attacking or defending his cynical view of women. He decided to expand his argument to convince his critics, although he conceded that when he referred to "all good-looking chicks", he was exaggerating. How could Paul go about convincing his readers that his personal impression has some basis in reality? A couple of students suggested that Paul follow Cosby's example and relate one of his own encounters with a woman. Do you think that approach would be effective?

Responder 2: Cindy ————————————————

Someone said that Cindy's response was a naive attempt to defend selfish women accused of abusing men. He considered Cindy's farfetched effort to excuse the girl's keeping Cosby's pin as proof that Cindy knew her position was indefensible. Quite a few other readers agreed with him, more or less. How might Cindy develop her belief that these women's seemingly cruel treatment of men covers a state of innocent confusion?

Responder 3: Margaret ————————————————

The choice for Margaret seemed to come down to (1) writing an account of her painful love affair with Matt, or (2) analyzing the motives of attractive people who take advantage of anyone who falls in love with them. Which option would you recommend, and why?

Rolf

SYLVIA ASHTON-WARNER

At school I found a new boy called Rolf Mannington, the same 1
age as me and who rode from across the Taura River on a fat sleek
pony, saddle too. A cared-for and handsome boy with clear sunned
skin, lovely grey eyes and a frequent friendly smile. From him to us all
there emanated a glamour that could not be ignored, a kind of mystery, my downfall. Even his name was interesting.

Yet he was unacceptable. He was too clever by half at his work, too 2
good-looking, too happy and with too pleasant a natural goodwill. Too
fortunate altogether. The mob doesn't like the exceptional; it distrusts
them to the point where it must destroy them. One lunchtime as we all
sat together beneath the pines, as we watched him open a splendid
lunch, we judged and convicted him on every count till resentment
reached flashpoint.

I don't know who started it but we ganged up and beat him, with 3
our fists first. We had to break the stranger open, expose his inside, kill
out that in him which was different from us and which we couldn't
understand. Defuse his mystery. The more he smiled as he sat on the
grass the more we hit him until, getting up, he struggled as far as the
horse-paddock fence to try to escape on his pony. But we held his coat
and he stuck in the wires thoroughly at our mercy. Compelled to remove the smile from him we picked up sticks and thrashed him.

We had to witness the fine one broken to see what he was made of, 4
to gloat on his private tears. We did see the fine one broken but not
what he was made of. True, the smile left his face and tears took its
place but we still could not identify the source of the glamour to eradi-
cate it. As Rolf cried and groaned and sagged in the wires the charisma
remained with him so that as we returned to the pines to our lunches,
gratified and justified, we only felt just as hungry for the food and
anything but satisfied.

Moreover, this new boy not only did not tell Teacher but turned up 5
the next morning exactly the same, his magnetism intact. The perfect
answer to persecution.

SAMPLE RESPONSES to "Rolf"

Responder 1: Carrie

Nobody likes someone who has everything. That is
why so many people like reading gossip magazines. They
feel much better when they see that rich and famous
people have serious personal problems and bad luck. They
are even happier when they see that someone who is
supposed to be very good turns out to be a crook or to
mistreat his family. A movie like Mommy Dearest draws
large audiences even though it is pretty stupid.
Everyone wants to see just how awful a beautiful woman
like Joan Crawford was to her child.

Responder 2: Leona

Children don't like goody-goodies because adults
always shower them with praise and special favors. A
teacher will say, "Why can't you all behave as well as
Rolf?" Popular children learn to keep their distance
from teachers even if they are good students. They make
sure to make a few mistakes in class and to misbehave
every once in a while.

Readers may think that the writer and her friends
were terribly cruel to Rolf, but this is probably quite
normal behavior. And Rolf learned something valuable
from the incident. He now understands the way most
people really feel.

Responder 3: Matthew ————————————————————

Why can't we accept goodness in others? It all begins with little children. When they are in a group, they become bullies and pick on those children who are somewhat different. This includes those who are very pleasant or very smart as well as those who are a little weird. Maybe kids don't get enough love at home, and that makes it hard for them to love others very much. So they envy anyone who seems really happy most of the time. It's like brothers and sisters; one is always thinking the other is getting more love and attention, and then hating them for it.

Responder 4: Migdalia ————————————————————

I knew a girl in junior high who was disliked by most of the students because she was very sweet and never took part in any activity that was the least bit bad. All the teachers thought Sarah was just splendid, and she constantly won awards. No one ever attacked her physically; in fact, she was elected class secretary; but everyone felt uncomfortable around her. Now she is studying to become a doctor and is planning to work with poor people in some part of the country where few doctors ever go.

My aunt says some people are too good for this world. Sarah and Rolf are like that. They are very confident of themselves and have no interest in doing things that are not right. The world needs more people like them, but

most of us don't really like such people because they
make us feel ashamed for not living up to our ideals.

Responder 5: Ronald ─────────────────────

The writer's final comment is absurd——"The perfect
answer to persecution." Is that what the Jews should
have done when the Nazis persecuted them? Most of them
did not resist, but the persecution went on. Are black
people supposed to come back the next day wearing a
smile after being beaten or insulted by bigots? They
accepted a hundred years of discrimination before
Martin Luther King showed them how to resist persecution
effectively. A century of humiliation was no "perfect
answer."

Of course, Rolf was different. He was a young god.
He seemed to belong to the master race. His refusal to
retaliate worked out well because the other children
envied him. In fact, his acceptance of the beating added
to his perfect image, for the other children wished they
could be so strong and cool in the face of adversity. For
Rolf, such a response was a "perfect answer." But it
would never work for the many victims of persecution in
this world.

CONSIDERING THE RESPONSES

Response 1: Carrie ─────────────────────

After reading or hearing about an act of cruelty, most people
attempt to explain it, to find an underlying cause. Carrie's response

represents such an effort to explain. She sees Rolf's beating as an example of how people envy someone who is blessed by good fortune. How would you advise Carrie to handle this idea in her essay? Should she present a series of examples to make her point, or should she just offer one major example of how envy affects people?

Response 2: Leona

Leona also wanted to examine the motive behind the attack, but she focused on a narrower topic, the children's dislike of the teacher's pet. Do you think Leona's approach, which covers less ground, is better than Carrie's? Why or why not? Can you suggest a good plan for Leona to follow in developing her essay? How would it differ from the approach you suggested for Carrie?

Response 3: Matthew

Matthew chose another path to explain the children's cruelty; he analyzed the event in social and psychological terms. Do you see a clear connection between children's tendency to bully those who are "different" and their jealousy of brothers or sisters who compete with them for parental love? Do you think Matthew can tie these two ideas together to create an effective essay? Or do you think Matthew would be better off developing just one of the ideas into an essay? Why?

Response 4: Migdalia

Migdalia's response covers a good deal of territory. Which of her ideas do you think Migdalia should choose for the main thesis of her longer essay? Why? Should Migdalia include the example of Sarah in her essay? If so, how much weight do you think she should give to it?

Response 5: Ronald

Ronald reacted not so much to the children's cruelty as to the writer's comment about the situation—the insight she hoped to convey to her readers. In fact, Ronald's response comes close to being a summary of a possible paper, for he had thought of several examples and has developed them fairly well. He has also described Rolf's situation at some length. What should Ronald do now to expand his ideas into an essay? Which of the ideas should he explore? Can he use all of them? Can you suggest an outline for Ronald to follow in writing his essay?

ADDITIONAL READINGS

Henri

GEORGE ORWELL

Or there was Henri, who worked in the sewers. He was a tall, melancholy man with curly hair, rather romantic-looking in his long, sewer-man's boots. Henri's peculiarity was that he did not speak, except for the purposes of work, literally for days together. Only a year before he had been a chauffeur in good employ and saving money. One day he fell in love, and when the girl refused him he lost his temper and kicked her. On being kicked the girl fell desperately in love with Henri, and for a fortnight they lived together and spent a thousand francs of Henri's money. Then the girl was unfaithful; Henri planted a knife in her upper arm and was sent to prison for six months. As soon as she had been stabbed the girl fell more in love with Henri than ever, and the two made up their quarrel and agreed that when Henri came out of jail he should buy a taxi and they would marry and settle down. But a fortnight later the girl was unfaithful again, and when Henri came out she was with child. Henri did not stab her again. He drew out all his savings and went on a drinking bout that ended in another month's imprisonment; after that he went to work in the sewers. Nothing would induce Henri to talk. If you asked him why he worked in the sewers he never answered, but simply crossed his wrists to signify handcuffs, and jerked his head southward, towards the prison. Bad luck seemed to have turned him half-witted in a single day.

Father

LANGSTON HUGHES

That summer in Mexico was the most miserable I have ever 1
known. I did not hear from my mother for several weeks. I did not like
my father. And I did not know what to do about either of them.

My father was what the Mexicans called *muy americano*, a typical 2
American. He was different from anybody I had ever known. He was
interested only in making money.

My mother and step-father were interested in making money, too, 3
so they were always moving about from job to job and from town to
town, wherever they heard times were better. But they were interested
in making money to *spend*. And for fun. They were always buying
victrolas and radios and watches and rings, and going to shows and
drinking beer and playing cards, and trying to have a good time after
working hours.

But my father was interested in making money to *keep*. 4

Because it is very hard for a Negro to make money in the United 5
States, since so many jobs are denied him, so many unions and professional associations are barred to him, so many banks will not advance
him loans, and so many insurance companies will not insure his business, my father went to Cuba and Mexico, where he could make money
quicker. He had had legal training in the South, but could not be admitted to the bar there. In Mexico he was admitted to the bar and
practiced law. He acquired property in Mexico City and a big ranch in
the hills. He lent money and foreclosed on mortgages.

During the revolutions, when all the white Americans had to flee 6
from the Toluca district of Mexico, because of the rising nationalism,
my father became the general manager of an electric light company
belonging to an American firm in New York. Because he was brown,
the Mexicans could not tell at sight that he was a Yankee, and even
after they knew it, they did not believe he was like the white Yankees.
So the followers of Zapata and Villa did not run him away as they did
the whites. In fact, in Toluca, the Mexicans always called my father *el
americano*, and not the less polite *el gringo*, which is a term that carries
with it distrust and hatred.

But my father was certainly just like the other German and English   7
and American business men with whom he associated in Mexico. He
spoke just as badly about the Mexicans. He said they were ignorant and
backward and lazy. He said they were exactly like the Negroes in the
United States, perhaps worse. And he said they were very bad at making money.

My father hated Negroes. I think he hated himself, too, for being a   8
Negro. He disliked all of his family because they were Negroes and
remained in the United States, where none of them had a chance to be
much of anything but servants—like my mother, who started out with a
good education at the University of Kansas, he said, but had sunk to
working in a restaurant, waiting on niggers, when she wasn't in some
white woman's kitchen. My father said he wanted me to leave the
United States as soon as I finished high school, and never return—
unless I wanted to be a porter or a red cap all my life.

The second day out from Cleveland, the train we were on rolled   9
across Arkansas. As we passed through a dismal village in the cotton
fields, my father peered from the window of our Pullman at a cluster
of black peons on the main street, and said contemptuously: "Look at
the niggers."

When we crossed into Mexico at Laredo, and started south over the   10
sun-baked plains, he pointed out to me a cluster of brown peons watching the train slow down at an adobe station. He said: "Look at the
Mexicans!"

My father had a great contempt for all poor people. He thought it   11
was their own fault that they were poor.

Our English Teacher

WILLIE MORRIS

Our English teacher was the wife of the owner of the barber 1
shop. She had grown up in a small town in Arkansas, and had even
spent some time in New York City before settling down in Mississippi.
In my first year in high school she lectured us for three weeks on An-
glo-Saxon England, and on the Normans, and then on Chaucer. She
made us take notes, because this was the way it was done in college, and
she said she wanted her students to go to college someday. She had us
read *The Canterbury Tales*, Shakespeare, George Eliot, Thackeray, and
Dickens, and Byron, Shelley, Keats, Coleridge, Wordsworth, Tennyson,
and Browning. Then she would have us give reports on the books and
poems we had read; woe to the unfortunate student who tried to mem-
orize the outlines of one of her novels by reading it in Classic Comics.
She was unsparing in her criticism, and she got rougher as we moved
into the higher grades. I must have parsed a hundred English sentences on the blackboard of that room, trying to come to reasonable
terms with gerundives, split infinitives, verb objects, and my own dangling prepositions. It was the one course in that school where great
quantities of homework were essential: novels, poems, themes, grammar, spelling. She would give the assignment at the end of every class,
and a big groan would fill the room. She would say, "Well, you want to
learn, don't you? Or maybe you *want* to stay saps all your life." She had
little patience with the slow ones, or the ones who refused to work, but
for those who tried, or who performed with some natural intelligence,
she was the most loyal and generous of souls. She would talk about
their virtues to everyone in town who would listen, and sometimes take
them home to have dinner with her and her husband and show them
colored pictures of the Lake Country or New England or Greenwich
Village.

Among many of the students she was a scorned woman. They bad- 2
talked her behind her back, tried to catch her in contradictions about
her travels, and rumored that she worked people that hard out of plain
cruelty; I myself sometimes joined in this talk, for it was fashionable.
Although she had been teaching there for many years, the students

61

never would dedicate the school yearbook to her, out of simple retalia-
tion, until my senior year when a friend and I managed to get the
dedication for her. In the school assembly when the dedication was
announced, her acceptance speech was a model of graciousness. She
talked about the honor that had been done her, and about the generation of students she had taught in the school, and about how she
wanted to stay there in Yazoo the rest of her life.

There must be many another small town in America with women   3
like her—trying, for whatever reason, to teach smalltown children the
hard basics of the language, and something of the literature it has produced—unyielding in their standards, despairing of mediocrity, and
incorruptible, and perhaps for all these reasons, scorned and misun-
derstood.

The Slanderer

ANTON CHEKHOV

Sergey Kapitonich Akhineyev, the teacher of calligraphy, gave 1
his daughter Natalya in marriage to the teacher of history and geography, Ivan Petrovich Loshadinikh. The wedding feast went on swim-
mingly. They sang, played, and danced in the parlor. Waiters, hired
for the occasion from the club, bustled about hither and thither like
madmen, in black frock coats and soiled white neckties. A loud noise of
voices smote the air. From the outside people looked in at the windows—their social standing gave them no right to enter.

Just at midnight the host, Akhineyev, made his way to the kitchen 2
to see whether everything was ready for the supper. The kitchen was
filled with smoke from the floor to the ceiling; the smoked reeked with
the odors of geese, ducks, and many other things. Victuals and bever-
ages were scattered about on two tables in artistic disorder. Marfa, the
cook, a stout, red-faced woman, was busying herself near the loaded
tables.

"Show me the sturgeon, dear," said Akhineyev, rubbing his hands 3
and licking his lips. "What a fine odor! I could just devour the whole
kitchen! Well, let me see the sturgeon!"

Marfa walked up to one of the benches and carefully lifted a greasy 4
newspaper. Beneath that paper, in a huge dish, lay a big fat sturgeon,
amid capers, olives, and carrots. Akhineyev glanced at the sturgeon
and heaved a sigh of relief. His face became radiant, his eyes rolled. He
bent down, and, smacking his lips, gave vent to a sound like a creaking
wheel. He stood a while, then snapped his fingers for pleasure, and
smacked his lips once more.

"Bah! The sound of a hearty kiss. Whom have you been kissing 5
there, Marfusha?" some one's voice was heard from the adjoining
room, and soon the closely cropped head of Vankin, the assistant
school instructor, appeared in the doorway. "Whom have you been
kissing here? A-a-ah! Very good! Sergey Kapitonich! A fine old man
indeed! With the female sex tête-à-tête!"

"I wasn't kissing at all," said Akhineyev, confused; "who told you, 6
you fool? I only—smacked my lips on account of—in consideration of
my pleasure—at the sight of the fish."

"Tell that to some one else, not to me!" exclaimed Vankin, whose 7
face expanded into a broad smile as he disappeared behind the door.
Akhineyev blushed.

"The devil knows what may be the outcome of this!" he thought. 8
"He'll go about tale-bearing now, the rascal. He'll disgrace me before
the whole town, the brute!"

Akhineyev entered the parlor timidly and cast furtive glances to see 9
what Vankin was doing. Vankin stood near the piano and, deftly bending down, whispered something to the inspector's sister-in-law, who was
laughing.

"That's about me!" thought Akhineyev. "About me, the devil take 10
him! She believes him, she's laughing. My God! No, that mustn't be left
like that. No. I'll have to fix it so that no one shall believe him. I'll speak
to all of them, and he'll remain a foolish gossip in the end."

Akhineyev scratched his head, and, still confused, walked up to 11
Padekoi.

"I was in the kitchen a little while ago, arranging things there for 12
the supper," he said to the Frenchman. "You like fish, I know, and I
have a sturgeon just so big. About two yards. Ha, ha, ha! Yes, by the
way, I have almost forgotten. There was a real anecdote about that
sturgeon in the kitchen. I entered the kitchen a little while ago and
wanted to examine the food. I glanced at the sturgeon and for pleasure, I smacked my lips—it was so piquant! And just at that moment the
fool Vankin entered and says—ha, ha, ha—and says: 'A-a! A-a-ah! You
have been kissing here?—with Marfa; just think of it—with the cook!
What a piece of invention, that blockhead, The woman is ugly, she
looks like a monkey, and he says we were kissing. What a queer fellow!"

"Who's a queer fellow?" asked Tarantulov, as he approached them. 13

"I refer to Vankin. I went out into the kitchen—" 14

The story of Marfa and the sturgeon was repeated. 15

"That makes me laugh. What a queer fellow he is. In my opinion it 16
is more pleasant to kiss the dog than to kiss Marfa," added Akhineyev,
and, turning around, he noticed Mzda.

"We have been speaking about Vankin," he said to him. "What a 17
queer fellow. He entered the kitchen and noticed me standing beside
Marfa, and immediately he began to invent different stories. 'What?' he
says, 'you have been kissing each other!' He was drunk, so he must
have been dreaming. 'And I,' I said, 'I would rather kiss a duck than
kiss Marfa. And I have a wife,' said I, 'you fool.' He made me appear
ridiculous."

"Who made you appear ridiculous?" inquired the teacher of reli- 18
gion, addressing Akhineyev.

"Vankin. I was standing in the kitchen, you know, and looking at 19
the sturgeon—" And so forth. In about half an hour all the guests
knew the story about Vankin and the sturgeon.

"Now let him tell," thought Akhineyev, rubbing his hands. "Let 20
him do it. He'll start to tell them, and they'll cut him short: 'Don't talk
nonsense, you fool! We know all about it.'"

And Akhineyev felt so much appeased that, for joy, he drank four 21
glasses of brandy over and above his fill. Having escorted his daughter
to her room, he went to his own and soon slept the sleep of an innocent
child, and on the following day he no longer remembered the story of
the sturgeon. But alas! Man proposes and God disposes. The evil
tongue does its wicked work, and even Akhineyev's cunning did not do
him any good. One week later, on a Wednesday, after the third lesson,
when Akhineyev stood in the teachers' room and discussed the vicious
inclinations of the pupil Visyekin, the director approached him, and,
beckoning to him, called him aside.

"See here, Sergey Kapitonich," said the director. "Pardon me. It 22
isn't my affair, yet I must make it clear to you, nevertheless. It is my
duty— You see, rumors are on foot that you are on intimate terms with
that woman—with your cook— It isn't my affair, but— You may be on
intimate terms with her, you may kiss her— You may do whatever you
like, but, please, don't do it so openly! I beg of you. Don't forget that
you are a pedagogue."

Akhineyev stood as though frozen and petrified. Like one stung by 23
a swarm of bees and scalded with boiling water, he went home. On his
way it seemed to him as though the whole town stared at him as at one
besmeared with tar— At home new troubles awaited him.

"Why don't you eat anything?" asked his wife at their dinner. 24
"What are you thinking about? Are you thinking about Cupid, eh? You
are longing for Marfushka. I know everything already, you Mahomet.
Kind people have opened my eyes, you barbarian!"

And she slapped him on the cheek. 25

He rose from the table, and staggering, without cap or coat, di- 26
rected his footsteps toward Vankin. The latter was at home.

"You rascal!" he said to Vankin. "Why have you covered me with 27
mud before the whole world? Why have you slandered me?"

"How; what slander? What are you inventing?" 28

"And who told everybody that I was kissing Marfa? Not you, per- 29
haps? Not you, you murderer?"

Vankin began to blink his eyes, and all the fibres of his face began 30
to quiver. He lifted his eyes toward the image and ejaculated:

"May God punish me, may I lose my eyesight and die, if I said even 31
a single word about you to any one! May I have neither house nor
home!"

Vankin's sincerity admitted of no doubt. It was evident that it was 32
not he who had gossiped.

"But who was it? Who?" Akhineyev asked himself, going over in his 33
mind all his acquaintances, and striking his chest. "Who was it?"

PART TWO

Responding to Situations and Events

The readings in Part Two are about situations and events that authors have found interesting or significant. They are likely to stimulate you to write about particular events or on-going situations that have affected your life or the lives of others. Based on your work with this book so far, however, you know that a reading arouses different responses in people. The best way to discover how an essay or story affects you is to record your strongest response as soon as you have finished reading it. Your response probably will contain the germ of an idea that matters to you and can form the basis of an essay that others will want to read.

Again, the first four readings of Part Two are followed by sample responses that should help you think about your own reaction to the essay or story. By considering these sample responses and answering the questions we ask, your own writing will become more effective. And don't forget to share your ideas with classmates and friends. Their reactions to your work will strengthen your writing.

You Should Have Been a Boy!

ELIZABETH CADY STANTON

When I was eleven years old, two events occurred which 1
changed considerably the current of my life. My only brother, who had
just graduated from Union College, came home to die. A young man
of great talent and promise, he was the pride of my father's heart. We
early felt that this son filled a larger place in our father's affections and
future plans than the five daughters together. Well do I remember
how tenderly he watched my brother in his last illness, the sighs and
tears he gave vent to as he slowly walked up and down the hall, and,
when the last sad moment came, and we were all assembled to say fare-
well in the silent chamber of death, how broken were his utterances as
he knelt and prayed for comfort and support. I still recall, too, going
into the large darkened parlor to see my brother, and finding the cas-
ket, mirrors, and pictures all draped in white, and my father seated by
his side, pale and immovable. As he took no notice of me, after standing a long while, I climbed upon his knee, when he mechanically put
his arm about me and, with my head resting against his beating heart,
we both sat in silence, he thinking of the wreck of all his hopes in the
loss of a dear son, and I wondering what could be said or done to fill
the void in his breast. At length he heaved a deep sigh and said: "Oh,
my daughter, I wish you were a boy!" Throwing my arms about his
neck, I replied: "I will try to be all my brother was."

Then and there I resolved that I would not give so much time as 2
heretofore to play, but would study and strive to be at the head of all
my classes and thus delight my father's heart. All that day and far into
the night I pondered the problem of boyhood. I thought that the chief
thing to be done in order to equal boys was to be learned and coura-
geous. So I decided to study Greek and learn to manage a horse. Having formed this conclusion I fell asleep. My resolutions, unlike many
such made at night, did not vanish with the coming light. I arose early
and hastened to put them into execution. They were resolutions never
to be forgotten—destined to mold my character anew. As soon as I was
dressed I hastened to our good pastor, Rev. Simon Hosack, who was
always early at work in his garden.

"Doctor," said I, "which do you like best, boys or girls?"   3

"Why, girls, to be sure; I would not give you for all the boys in   4
Christendom."

"My father," I replied, "prefers boys; he wishes I was one, and I   5
intend to be as near like one as possible. I am going to ride on horseback and study Greek. Will you give me a Greek lesson now, doctor? I
want to begin at once."

"Yes, child," said he, throwing down his hoe, "come into my library   6
and we will begin without delay."

He entered fully into the feeling of suffering and sorrow which   7
took possession of me when I discovered that a girl weighed less in the
scale of being than a boy, and he praised my determination to prove
the contrary. The old grammar which he had studied in the University
of Glasgow was soon in my hands, and the Greek article was learned
before breakfast.

Then came the sad pageantry of death, the weeping of friends, the   8
dark rooms, the ghostly stillness, the exhortation to the living to prepare for death, the solemn prayer, the mournful chant, the funeral
cortège, the solemn, tolling bell, the burial. How I suffered during
those sad days! What strange undefined fears of the unknown took
possession of me! For months afterward, at the twilight hour, I went
with my father to the new-made grave. Near it stood two tall poplar
trees, against one of which I leaned, while my father threw himself on
the grave, with outstretched arms, as if to embrace his child. At last the
frosts and storms of November came and threw a chilling barrier between the living and the dead, and we went there no more.

During all this time I kept up my lessons at the parsonage and   9
made rapid progress. I surprised even my teacher, who thought me
capable of doing anything. I learned to drive, and to leap a fence and
ditch on horseback. I taxed every power, hoping some day to hear my
father say: "Well, a girl is as good as a boy, after all." But he never said
it. When the doctor came over to spend the evening with us, I would
whisper in his ear: "Tell my father how fast I get on," and he would tell
him, and was lavish in his praises. But my father only paced the room,
sighed, and showed that he wished I were a boy; and I, not knowing
why he felt thus, would hide my tears of vexation on the doctor's shoulder.

Soon after this I began to study Latin, Greek, and mathematics   10
with a class of boys in the Academy, many of whom were much older
than I. For three years one boy kept his place at the head of the class,
and I always stood next. Two prizes were offered in Greek. I strove for
one and took the second. How well I remember my joy in receiving
that prize. There was no sentiment of ambition, rivalry, or triumph
over my companions, nor feeling of satisfaction in receiving this honor

in the presence of those assembled on the day of the exhibition. One thought alone filled my mind. "Now," said I, "my father will be satisfied with me." So, as soon as we were dismissed, I ran down the hill, rushed breathless into his office, laid the new Greek Testament, which was my prize, on his table and exclaimed: "There, I got it!" He took up the book, asked me some questions about the class, the teachers, the spectators, and evidently pleased, handed it back to me. Then, while I stood looking and waiting for him to say something which would show that he recognized the equality of the daughter with the son, he kissed me on the forehead and exclaimed, with a sigh, "Ah, you should have been a boy!"

SAMPLE RESPONSES to "You Should Have Been a Boy!"

Responder 1: Celia

What a father! How could he be so mean to his daughter! She tried to take the place of the son, but the father didn't care. All he wanted was the boy. I'm glad my father is different. He tells me I'm the one who should continue my education because I do well in school. He tells my brother that he should start thinking about learning some sort of trade because "Ronnie and books don't get along." If the father in the story had been more like my father, the girl would have been appreciated for what she did. Ugh! What a father!

Responder 2: Leona

It's the same old story. Boys are the pride and joy of the family, while girls are just supposed to be nice, get married, and not have any ambitions about being

somebody. That's the way my family reacts to me. I told
my mother the other night that I was thinking about
becoming a doctor. I didn't tell her that I was certain
since I know that it isn't easy to become a doctor. I
only said I was thinking about it. She just sort of
smiled and said that I'd probably change my mind when I
met some nice fellow. I felt like screaming, but my
mother, even though she's not that old, was brought up
in a very traditional family. So, for her, a woman's
place is in the kitchen. On the other hand, when my
brother told my father he wanted to be a physical
therapist, my father got mad and said he was aiming too
low. He thinks my brother has what it takes to be a
doctor. When I asked my father, "What about me?" he said
that only certain women are able to do it—become
doctors, he meant. In other words, only superwomen can
compete with men when it comes to the higher jobs. The
whole thing drives me up the wall, but there's not much I
can do about it right now.

Responder 3: Sonia

I know the other women in the class will make a big
thing out of this essay. They'll talk about women's lib
and how men have kept women suppressed all through
history. As a woman I should probably agree with them,
but my experiences tell me different. When I was ten
years old, my mother decided that being a housewife and
mother wasn't good enough. She wanted a career, and she

wanted to earn her own money. My father had a good job, and so we really didn't need extra money. But my mother kept saying that she didn't want to spend the rest of her life trapped in a house. So my mother got a job selling real estate, which she liked. She liked her job so much that she came home late almost every night. And all she ever talked about was how exciting her job was and how she was working her way up the ladder. All this was fine for her, but it wasn't fine for me.

I had to take over her housework. My brother was five years old at the time, and so I had to be a mother for him. My father would come home hungry from work, and I had to cook for him, even though I wasn't very good at it. My father tried to help, but he wasn't much of a cook either, and besides, he was usually too tired. My life became a mess. I couldn't go out with my friends or even spend much time talking to my friends on the phone or watching TV. The whole thing ended in a divorce, which I don't even like to think about. But you can see why I'm not so sure about women's lib.

Responder 4: Randy

God set up the way men and women should live. When people try to live their own way and not God's way, things go wrong. The daughter tried to be a boy, which was wrong. God created her a woman, and she tried to be a man. That's why her father said what he said. He knew she could not change God's plan for her. True, if she had been a boy, then what she did would have been all right. But wanting to be a different sex than you are is a sin.

A lot of the problems in the world today are caused by women trying to act like men. Instead of being mothers and housewives as God intended them to be, they want to do the work that God intended men to do. That's why so many young people are on drugs or are involved in all kinds of crime and violence. These kids don't know right from wrong. How could they, when their mothers don't know right from wrong? If women don't start acting the way God made them to act, there's a lot more trouble coming to this world.

CONSIDERING THE RESPONSES

Response 1: Celia

Celia compared her father's attitude toward her academic success with the attitude of Elizabeth Cady Stanton's father toward Elizabeth's success. An obvious strategy for Celia in planning an essay might be to expand on the portrait of her father as a person who understands and appreciates his daughter's academic success. If Celia decides to follow this strategy, how might she develop her essay? During class discussion of Celia's response, several students took exception to what they saw as a "put down" of Celia's brother by his father. These students were disturbed by the implication that learning a trade is somehow inferior to doing well in school. Is there a possible essay topic in the feelings these students expressed? How would you summarize that topic?

Response 2: Leona

Leona evidently feels that, because she is female, her parents do not take her career aspirations seriously. She complains that her mother's attitude toward her reflects her mother's traditional upbringing. If Leona decides to write an essay that might help readers get a clear idea of just what it's like to grow up in a "traditional" family, how might she relate her topic to Elizabeth Cady Stanton's piece?

Response 3: Sonia

Some students felt that Sonia's rather lengthy response put her well on the way to writing a complete essay, and they suggested that all she needed to do was to provide more detail about the "misery" she went through because of her mother's decision to pursue a career. Other students, however, thought that Sonia was somewhat unfair to her mother. They asked whether something about the father's attitude prevented the couple from working out a satisfactory plan that would have relieved Sonia of the housework at the same time it allowed her mother to pursue her career. If Sonia does decide to explore the breakup of the family, how much of her initial response do you think she can use in her essay? Which ideas would still fit the new topic? If Sonia decides to stay with her original response, does she need to add details about the hard life she led in order to make a strong case for her personal objection to women's liberation or has she already proved her case in her original response?

Response 4: Randy

Randy takes a truly traditional view of the events Elizabeth Cady Stanton described. Do you think Randy can support his idea that God set up the way men and women should live? What kind of supporting details should he offer to convince readers that he is correct? What questions might some readers raise about Randy's belief that much of the trouble in the world results from women's trying to act "like men"? Do you think Randy can develop an essay based on the ideas expressed in his original response? Why or why not?

Salvation

LANGSTON HUGHES

I was saved from sin when I was going on thirteen. But not really 1
saved. It happened like this. There was a big revival at my Auntie
Reed's church. Every night for weeks there had been much preaching,
singing, praying, and shouting, and some very hardened sinners had
been brought to Christ, and the membership of the church had grown
by leaps and bounds. Then just before the revival ended, they held a
special meeting for children, "to bring the young lambs to the fold."
My aunt spoke of it for days ahead. That night I was escorted to the
front row and placed on the mourners' bench with all the other young
sinners, who had not yet been brought to Jesus.

My aunt told me that when you were saved you saw a light, and 2
something happened to you inside! And Jesus came into your life! And
God was with you from then on! She said you could see and hear and
feel Jesus in your soul. I believed her. I have heard a great many old
people say the same thing and it seemed to me they ought to know. So
I sat there calmly in the hot, crowded church, waiting for Jesus to come
to me.

The preacher preached a wonderful rhythmical sermon, all moans 3
and shouts and lonely cries and dire pictures of hell, and then he sang
a song about the ninety and nine safe in the fold, but one little lamb was
left out in the cold. Then he said: "Won't you come? Won't you come
to Jesus? Young lambs, won't you come?" And he held out his arms to
all us young sinners there on the mourners' bench. And the little girls
cried. And some of them jumped up and went to Jesus right away. But
most of us just sat there.

A great many old people came and knelt around us and prayed, 4
old women with jet-black faces and braided hair, old men with work-
gnarled hands. And the church sang a song about the lower lights are
burning, some poor sinners to be saved. And the whole building
rocked with prayer and song.

Still I kept waiting to *see* Jesus. 5

Finally all the young people had gone to the altar and were saved, 6
but one boy and me. He was a rounder's son named Westley. Westley

75

and I were surrounded by sisters and deacons praying. It was very hot in the church, and getting late now. Finally Westley said to me in a whisper: "God damn! I'm tired o' sitting here. Let's get up and be saved." So he got up and was saved.

Then I was left all alone on the mourners' bench. My aunt came   7
and knelt at my knees and cried, while prayers and songs swirled all around me in the little church. The whole congregation prayed for me alone, in a mighty wail of moans and voices. And I kept waiting serenely for Jesus, waiting, waiting—but he didn't come. I wanted to see him, but nothing happened to me. Nothing! I wanted something to happen to me, but nothing happened.

I heard the songs and the minister saying: "Why don't you come?   8
My dear child, why don't you come to Jesus? Jesus is waiting for you. He wants you. Why don't you come? Sister Reed, what is the child's name?"

"Langston," my aunt sobbed.   9

"Langston, why don't you come? Why don't you come and be   10
saved? Oh, Lamb of God! Why don't you come?"

Now it was really getting late. I began to be ashamed of myself,   11
holding everything up so long. I began to wonder what God thought about Westley, who certainly hadn't seen Jesus either, but who was now sitting proudly on the platform, swinging his knickerbockered legs and grinning down at me, surrounded by deacons and old women on their knees praying. God had not struck Westley dead for taking his name in vain or for lying in the temple. So I decided that maybe to save further trouble, I'd better lie, too, and say that Jesus had come, and get up and be saved.

So I got up.   12

Suddenly the whole room broke into a sea of shouting, as they saw   13
me rise. Waves of rejoicing swept the place. Women leaped in the air. My aunt threw her arms around me. The minister took me by the hand and led me to the platform.

When things quieted down, in a hushed silence, punctuated by a   14
few ecstatic "Amens," all the new young lambs were blessed in the name of God. Then joyous singing filled the room.

That night, for the last time in my life but one—for I was a big boy   15
twelve years old—I cried. I cried, in bed alone, and couldn't stop. I buried my head under the quilts, but my aunt heard me. She woke up and told my uncle I was crying because the Holy Ghost had come into my life, and because I had seen Jesus. But I was really crying because I couldn't bear to tell her that I had lied, that I had deceived everybody in the church, that I hadn't seen Jesus, and that now I didn't believe there was a Jesus any more, since he didn't come to help me.

SAMPLE RESPONSES to "Salvation"

Responder 1: Joel _____

I hate it when people expect me to perform. When I was a little boy, my mother wanted me to thank my aunt for an ugly sweater that only a girl would wear. She told me to go over and make a little speech. I ran upstairs and hid, and later I was punished for being rude. And when I was in seventh grade, the teacher chose me to recite a poem on Parents Day. I couldn't face standing up in front of all those people, and so I stayed home pretending I was sick. You have to let people do things on their own and not force them.

Responder 2: Erika _____

Religion is for hypocrites, as Langston Hughes so rightly states. That revival meeting was packed with persons just like Westley. But the others were quicker than Westley and Langston to catch on and play the game. When anyone goes along with religion by saying they love Jesus or any other deity, they feel they need to force everyone else to join their club so that no one will know they were lying. Eventually, they begin to believe what they are saying because they say it so often. As history has shown, these groups of believers often become angry that not everyone agrees with them, and they go to war to force the rest of the world to say that their way is the right way. Most of the problems in this world can be traced to some people trying to make other people accept their religion.

Responder 3: Clark

Life presents us with many problems which we cannot cope with alone without divine assistance. I was miserable when I was in high school. No one liked me, and I was always in a lot of trouble. My parents said I was no good, and it was all because I had not found Our Lord. I was arrested when I was seventeen, and I guess that scared me enough to think about what I was doing to myself. My sister had been trying to get me to go to meetings, and I finally did. At first I was most uncomfortable because all the other people seemed so good. But one time I heard people confessing their sinful ways and telling how they had found peace, and I began to feel something inside. When I finally took Our Lord to me, I knew my troubles were over. Now I am happy, and I'll never be unable to face any problems that come along.

Responder 4: John

Langston Hughes was the only honest one. He admitted to himself that he had lied—about seeing Jesus. I bet everybody in that church lied too.

Everybody went along with the show, though, because
nobody wanted to be different. When you're different,
people go against you or think you're weird. I'll bet
half the students in this college don't want to be here,
but are just conforming to what their parents want or
what society wants. At least Langston had the guts to
hold out until the crowd almost went crazy. I don't
think I could have held out that long.

CONSIDERING THE RESPONSES

Response 1: Joel

Joel's experiences were quite different from the author's, but they represent a topic that holds great interest for him. When the class asked him how he planned to create an essay from this response, he said he remembered other embarrassing times when he was under pressure to perform, and he could add more details to the two incidents already mentioned. The class advised him to discuss at some length the general situation—adults forcing children to do something that seems "good" or "right." Should Joel's essay include a look at the situation from the adults' point of view? Or should he stick to his own feelings and what he supposes other children would have felt? Depending on your answer to question 1, advise Joel about how to plan his essay.

Response 2: Erika

Erika faced the opposite problem from Joel, for she had too many wide-reaching ideas for a short essay. The other students noticed that Erika's response contained two rather large topics: (1) her view that most religious people are hypocrites and (2) her ideas about religious wars. Which of the two topics do you think would be easier to develop into an effective essay? Why? Depending on your answer to question 1, what kinds of supporting detail should Erika include?

Response 3: Clark _____

Clark's response contained plenty of material for an essay, and
the class thought that his essay could be divided into three major
sections. What three sections do you think the class found in Clark's
response? Should Clark develop all three sections in his essay or focus
on only one or two? Why?

Response 4: John _____

John's response triggered a lively discussion about the issue of
conformity. The class was especially interested in John's contention
that half the students in the school didn't want to be there. What
ideas in "Salvation" caused John to write about college rather than
religion? Is John's response closely connected to Langston Hughes's
piece? Why or why not?

Unresolved Grief: Drowning in Life's Debris

SUE PATTON THOELE

All of us experience grief. We have small losses: rain on a vaca- 1
tion, gaining 10 pounds; and large losses: the loss of a job, illness, the
death of a child.

A recent study measured the chemicals in tears. Those shed in hap- 2
piness, awe, or other positive emotions were toxin-free, while tears
shed in frustration, anger, fear, or grief had a significant poison-con-
tent.

Tears cleanse and heal. We need to weep over the discrepancies in 3
our lives—the difference between our dreams and reality. All of us feel
our losses and disappointments, but few of us feel free to grieve fully.
A chasm of unresolved grief lies festering in our hearts.

Our local Hospice chapter has bereavement groups, which I lead. 4
The people in these groups have all lost a person close to them. Some
join the group while the loss is still very fresh in their minds and hearts.
Naturally, their feelings are raw and excruciating. Many cry—and most
apologize for doing so. Yet what could be more natural or healing than
to weep for a grievous loss?

In our society, we feel we need to apologize for our tears, even for 5
our feelings. There is good reason for this. Until recently neither society nor friends encouraged us to express feelings of grief. How many
times have you heard someone say, "John is taking the death of his son
so well." What that probably means is that John has suppressed his
feelings and isn't acting out his suffering in front of others. As a society
of "fixers," we are uncomfortable with another's un-fixable pain.

We resolve our discomfort by simply avoiding people who are ex- 6
periencing pain. People who've gone through a divorce frequently tell
me, "So many of my friends avoid me now." It's not that divorce ren-
ders you socially unacceptable; it's that friends can't "fix" it and don't
know how to deal with the pain of the parties concerned, or with what
it stirs up in themselves.

We're encouraged to let our grief sit, silent and unresolved, in the 7 pit of our soul, where it becomes part of the dragged-around debris of our life. The *American Heritage Dictionary* defines "debris" as ". . . the scattered remains of something broken or destroyed; ruins, rubble, fragments . . ." I call it: "left-over stuff, unfinished business, old feelings that have never been healed."

Grief comes in many forms. Grief over death and loss is just one 8 form. Another is grief over the things we feel we should have done or shouldn't have done. When we fight with friends or mates, we grieve. When too many bills pile up and money is tight, we grieve. Anything unfinished and left to fester becomes emotional debris, the litter of unresolved grief. Debris is a mountain of garbage that stands in the path of our lives.

How can we collect that which is "scattered or broken" in our lives? 9 Imagine a home in which no one ever swept up the fragments of broken dishes, no one ever took out the garbage, or used the disposal. In a very short while, that house would be uninhabitable. No one could live like that! (Except my son and daughter, when they were teenagers.)

The point is, many of us allow emotional debris to collect in our 10 hearts, minds, and souls. Soon the mounds of dirt that we've swept under our emotional carpets become too big to ignore. They keep us from walking around freely in our own inner homes and separate us from those we care about. Those mounds of hidden debris soon erode our freedom to make conscious choices regarding how we will feel and act.

SAMPLE RESPONSES to "Unresolved Grief"

Responder 1: Elvira

My mother died a year and a half ago. We were a close family—my mother, my father, my brother, Ricky, and me. My brother and I cried every day for weeks. We couldn't believe that our mother was really gone and would never come back.

My father never cried. He looked sad. He kept going to work every day. But he never cried and he never talked about my mother. He has been living like a man with no life in him. My brother and I have accepted the fact that our mother is dead. We still feel sad at times, and we sometimes talk about Mother and cry. But mostly we have accepted her death and are going on with our lives.

My father, however, just won't snap out of it. He says he'll be all right, but I'm worried about him. I'm going to give him this essay to read. I hope it helps him to see that he can't go on as he has.

Responder 2: Rudy

Maybe people handle grief in different ways. I don't see where a person has to go around crying all over the place or telling everybody his troubles. Maybe a person wants to keep his grief to himself. It doesn't mean he's not handling his grief. It means that he's handling it in his own way. If a person wants to cry a lot and tell everyone his troubles, fine. Let him do it if it helps. If a person doesn't want to cry about his grief or talk about it, that's fine too, as long as he's able to cope. People don't do things in the same way. So I don't see why everybody has to grieve in the same way, the way these authors want us to.

Responder 3: Florence

I'm in my mid-forties and I'm just now taking my first college courses. It's a bit scary being back in school after so many years but I'm glad I'm here. Before

I came back to school I was suffering from depression. I
felt that I had let my life slip away without doing
anything that I could be proud of. As this essay says, I
was suffering grief over something that I thought I
should have done. I was in therapy quite a while before I
came to realize that it does you no good to live in the
past. I threw out the "emotional debris" of my past and
decided to start life anew. Now I'll live for the
present and for the future. The past is gone. I'm glad
that I finally got rid of it.

Responder 4: Terrence

What's this world coming to! Here we have so-called
experts who want us to treat grief as if it were no more
of a problem than the debris in a dirty house. Emotional
debris! Is that what pain, anguish and suffering are
called in this modern world? Yes, grief is terrible, but
grief and suffering are a part of life. We can't
eliminate grief simply by crying and talking. These
days, everybody wants to sell us instant cures. Have a
headache? Take a pill. Can't sleep? Take this drug. No
need to deal with problems and pain anymore. Feeling
grief? Just sweep that dirty grief out of your mind and
go on living as if nothing had happened. What nonsense!
People who grow stronger as individuals don't look for
instant relief. People who grow in emotional maturity
take on grief, face up to it, and become stronger
through their suffering.

CONSIDERING THE RESPONSES

Responder 1: Elvira

Elvira relates a very personal experience in her response to the essay. She contrasts her reactions and those of her brother to her father's reactions and implies thereby that the advice given in the essay is good advice. Some students thought that a more detailed essay by Elvira would prove interesting and helpful to others. Other students thought that Elvira had a possible essay in writing about her father's reactions to the author's advice, provided that Elvira could get her father to read and respond to the essay. How might Elvira consider both possibilities in her essay?

Responder 2: Rudy

Rudy's response indicates that he doesn't accept the idea that there is only one way to overcome grief. How can Rudy support his argument, which runs somewhat counter to the advice offered in the essay? Would just one or two examples of people he knows who have overcome grief by holding it in be enough to convince readers that silent grief is also a viable response to tragedy or bad luck? What other methods might Rudy use to support his point of view?

Responder 3: Florence

Florence's experiences seem to have inclined her to accept the advice given in the essay. In this regard, she makes a particular point of responding positively to the author's point that we can feel grief over things we feel we should have done in the past. Despite her statement that she is glad that she finally got rid of her past, some students suggested that she take a look back. They felt that she was being too hard on herself by saying that she had done nothing that she could be proud of. If Florence accepts this advice, would she have to limit her review of the past? What suggestions could you make to her about how to limit the ideas she would discuss in such an essay?

Responder 4: Terrence ———————————————————

Terrence was apparently upset by the essay, as can be seen by his comparing the author's advice to "instant relief." In class discussion, students were confused about the point Terrence wanted to make. What would Terrence have to do in order to clarify his response in a longer, organized essay? What do you think would be his main problem in writing such an essay?

A Real Loss

FERN KUPFER

I was sitting in back of a little girl flying as an unaccompanied minor, put on the plane by a mother who placed a Care Bear in her arms and told her to remind Daddy to call when she got to California. The girl adjusted her seat belt and sniffed back a tear, bravely setting her jaw.

As we prepared for takeoff, the man next to the girl asked her the name of her bear and nodded in approval, saying Furry was a good name for a bear. When the little girl told him she was 6 years old, the man replied that he had a daughter who was 6 years old. His daughter was missing the same teeth, in fact. He asked how much money the tooth fairy was giving out in New York these days.

By the time we were in the air, the man and the little girl were playing tic-tac-toe, and she revealed to him the names of her favorite friends. Somewhere over Ohio, I fell asleep, awakened by my mother instinct when I heard a child announce that she had to go to the bathroom.

"It's in the back, right?" I heard the girl say to the man. She looked tentative. The flight attendants were busy collecting lunch trays.

"Do you want me to take you there?" the man asked, standing.

At once my antennae were up and, leaning into the aisle, I craned my neck, practically knocking heads with the woman in the seat across from me. For one moment our eyes locked. She had been listening, too, and both of us had the same idea. Would this man go into the bathroom with the child? I held my breath as he held open the bathroom door. Suddenly, he became transformed in my eyes—the dark business suit looked sinister, the friendly smile really a lure to something evil.

Then the man showed the little girl how the lock worked and waited outside the door. The woman and I sighed in relief. She said, "Well, you can't be too careful these days."

I've thought about that man on the plane since then, and the image of him and the little girl always leaves an empty sorrow. I know that a new heightened consciousness about child molestation is in itself a good thing. I know that sexual abuse of children is awful, and that we must guard against it. But it saddened me that I looked at someone who understood a child's fear and saw a child molester.

These are trying times for men. We women say how we want men to be sensitive and nurturing, to be caring and affectionate. But my sense is that now these qualities cannot be readily displayed without arousing suspicion. Perhaps there is some sort of ironic retribution for all those years of accepting the male stereotypes. But there is a real loss here for us all when we must always be wary of the kindness of strangers.

SAMPLE RESPONSES to "A Real Loss"

Responder 1: Ben _____

I guess this lady is right about everyone becoming suspicious of each other now that we have learned about various kinds of abuse. My mother went through a terrible experience with the Child Protection Agency when my little brother fell out of his bunk bed one night and came up with a black eye and several bruises that became visible when he was in gym class the next day. Buddy has always been a bit clumsy, so he often goes to school with a bump or a bandage, but these were all due to accidents, not to parental abuse. Buddy has no interest in sports, and he avoids getting into fights. These facts may have caused the teachers to suspect he had been beaten. However, they should not have called the agency; they should have accepted Buddy's explanation, which Mom confirmed. The social worker accused Mom of neglect because she works and that means my sister and brother are home alone after school until dinner. I think all this reporting on other people sounds a lot like a police state.

Responder 2: Jerry

This lady is a professional snoop who is always trying to find fault with her neighbors. In the "good old days" she refers to, she would have been just as nosey and critical, only then she would have gone after the mother who placed the little girl on the plane. "All alone—just think of it! What's the world coming to these days?" Of course, then someone might have criticized her obnoxious behavior by pointing out that the girl could not visit her father very often unless the parents were wealthy enough for each one to fly with her and return alone, both ways. Today this woman can get away with her snooping by saying she is "just doing her duty as a citizen. Haven't you seen all those perverts on the TV news?"

Responder 3: Shirley

Most of us have been sensitized in recent years by newspapers and TV to the horrible crime of child abuse. At first I thought the media were exploiting the situation by calling so much attention to an isolated case, here and there. Those reports of mentally ill parents injuring their helpless children made my blood run cold, and I felt ashamed for being fascinated by

pictures of the pitiful victims on television. And then
there came the TV docudramas depicting the crimes and
asking us viewers to stop minding our own business when
an adult swatted his or her child in public. We were told
to step into the scene and calmly try to help the abuser
see how wrong it is to strike children in anger.

Sounded like the right advice at the time, but then
one day I witnessed a rather tough looking woman in the
A & P shouting at her little girl and then slapping her
across the back of her head, hard! Bravely I intervened,
fearing she would hit the child again, this time for
crying at having been struck. I tried to be diplomatic,
but the woman roared at me, spewing out obscenities. And
she didn't stop. The manager came over and pushed me
away, telling me to mind my own business. I was outraged
at him, but when I looked for support from the other
shoppers, they all looked the other way. One woman later
told me I was wrong because the violent scene probably
embarrassed and scared the girl more than having been
hit for whatever she had done that irritated her mother.
I felt miserable; what a fool I had been.

A few weeks later, I read an article that advised us
crusaders to be more subtle. We should tell the abuser
that we understand how upsetting children can be, and
that we have felt just as angry as she must feel, many
times. However, we have found that it doesn't help to
hit them, etc, etc, etc. That convinced me that these
media psychologists pose a clear and present danger to
people like me, who want to do the right thing. None of
them seems to understand the common man, or woman. Their

idiotic advice is almost certain to produce dreadful
scenes, like the one I went through. I'll wait until I
see an adult beating a child with a baseball bat before I
interfere again, and even then I'll have second
thoughts.

CONSIDERING THE RESPONSES

Responder 1: Ben

The class divided evenly over the best topic for Ben. Some felt he should tell his brother's story in full detail, using the incident to illustrate the idea that appearances can be deceiving, and therefore well-meaning people need to move cautiously in cases such as Buddy's. Other students recommended that he write an editorial condemning the social workers and the school for their abuse of a working mother. Which approach do you think would produce a better essay? Why?

Responder 2: Jerry

At first Jerry's classmates were surprised by his response, and some accused him of being much too negative. But as they discussed his impression of the woman on the plane, some saw his point and urged him to work on the idea further. Do you see a way for Jerry to develop an essay out of his reaction to the woman who feared the male passenger might abuse the child?

Responder 3: Shirley

Her response was so complete that no one had much advice to offer Shirley. Some questioned her distrust of psychologists. They believed Shirley had been unfortunate to come across a truly violent woman. They suggested that Shirley tell her story but leave off the criticism of the psychologists. Do you agree with this advice? Explain your position.

ADDITIONAL READINGS

Your Eyes Can Deceive You

ARTHUR BARTLETT

George Smith got home from a date with his girl about midnight. His mother was not at home. Probably she was out playing cards with friends, George thought. That had been her favorite recreation ever since her divorce, when George was six. Working all day in the candy factory, she liked to relax in the evenings. Now that George was 20, and working, and had a girl to occupy his attention, she often stayed out fairly late. So George went up to his own front room, undressed, got into bed and lay there reading the newspaper. 1

A bus stopped across the street, and George pulled aside the window shade and looked out. Under the street light, he could see his mother descending from the bus. A tall, heavy-set man got out behind her. The bus moved on. George was about to drop back on his pillow when his startled eyes stopped him. The man was reaching for his mother, trying to put his arms around her. George saw her push at him and try to step back off the curb; saw him grab her again and start pulling her towards him. 2

George leaped out of bed, pulled on his trousers and rushed down the stairs to the front door. Across the street, the man was still attempting to embrace his mother and she was struggling against him. George dashed to the rescue. Clenching his fist as he ran, he leaped at the man and punched with all his strength, hitting him squarely on the jaw. The man topped backward and uttered a groan as his head hit the sidewalk. Then he lay there, still. 3

What happened next filled George with utter confusion. Dropping 4

92

to her knees beside the unconscious man, his mother looked up at him with anguish in her eyes. "George," she cried, "what have you done? This is Howard Browser. . . . Howard, the candymaker at the factory . . . the man who asked me to marry him." . . .

The boy stared at his mother across the crumpled figure on the ⁵ pavement. "He wasn't attacking you?" he demanded, dully.

"Of course not," she told him. "We'd been out together all evening. ⁶ He brought me home. He wanted a good-night kiss, that's all. I was just teasing him."

An ambulance took Howard Browser to the hospital, but he never ⁷ regained consciousness. He died the next day. George Smith spent that night in a jail cell.

The authorities finally decided not to prosecute. George, the inves- ⁸ tigation proved, didn't know Browser; had never seen him before. He had honestly thought that what he saw was a man attacking his mother.

But he had been misled by what he saw. His imagination exagger- ⁹ ated the evidence presented by his own eyes and converted it into something that wasn't true at all. As a result he had killed his mother's suitor. . . .

There's Only Luck

RUTH REICHL

My mind went numb when I saw the gun pointing against the 1
car window as we pulled out of the garage: This can't be happening to
me. Then I felt the gun, cold, against my head, and I heard my friend
Jeremy saying, "What do you want? Take my wallet," but at the time
nothing registered. I didn't question why they wanted us to go into the
house; only later did I realize that there must have been more than
money on their minds.

I remember being only vaguely annoyed when the man with the 2
gun pulled me from the car by my hair, and annoyed at being called a
bitch. I remember the walk up to the house and, behind us, Jeremy
and another man with a gun. I remember the fear and anger in both
men's voices because Jeremy was being so slow, and I remember wondering *why* he was being so slow. I did not realize that Jeremy had
thrown the keys into the shrubbery, but I do remember Jeremy sinking
to his knees saying, "I'm sorry, I'm sorry." And I remember the sound
of the gun hitting Jeremy's head and the feeling as the man who had
hold of my hair released me. And I remember the split second when I
realized that he had not only let go of me but that he was looking at
Jeremy and the man who was hitting him, and I remember that tiny
question in my mind about how far I could run, how fast and how
likely it was that I could make it to the car parked across the street
before he pulled the trigger. But I was already running as I thought
these things, and when I got to the car I didn't crouch behind it but
screamed instead.

I remember thinking that there was something absurdly melodra- 3
matic about screaming, "Help, help!" at eight o'clock on a Tuesday evening in December in the Hollywood Hills, and then seeing, in my mind,
the man behind me with the gun, and changing my plea to a more
specific one. "Help, let me in, *please* let me in!" But the houses were
cold, closed, unfriendly, and I ran on until I saw a screen door, thinking that I could leap right through it if I had to. But by then I had
heard Jeremy's screams behind me, and I knew that our attackers had
fled.

The neighbors who had not opened their doors to us came out 4
with baseball bats and helped Jeremy find his glasses and keys. In a
group they were very brave. We waited for the cops to come, until
someone said to someone else that the fettuccine was getting cold, and
I said politely, "Please go and eat. I'm all right."

I was happy to see the neighbors go. They had been talking of 5
stiffer sentences, of bringing back the death penalty and how Reagan is
going to clean up the country. I was thinking, they could be saying all
of this over my dead body, and I *still* feel that stiffer sentences wouldn't
change a thing. All the rage I should have felt for my attackers came
out in a rush against these complacent people standing in front of their
snug homes talking about all the guns they were going to buy. What
good would guns have been to us?

People all over the neighborhood had called to report our screams, 6
and the police turned out in force. When the cops arrived twenty minutes later they were grumpy and disgusted at so much ado about what
was, to them, nothing. After all, Jeremy was hardly hurt, and we were
hopeless when it came to identification. "Typical," snorted one cop
when we couldn't even agree on how tall the men were. Both of us
were able to describe the guns in horrifying detail, but the two policemen who stayed to make the report didn't think that would be much
help.

The cops were matter-of-fact about the whole thing. The fat one 7
went off to take a call, and his thin partner took our depositions. "That
was a stupid thing to do," he said, "throwing away the keys. When a
man has a gun against your head you do what you're told." Jeremy
looked properly sheepish.

Then the fat cop came back, and the thin one went off to prowl 8
around the house, "That was the best thing you could have done,
throwing away your keys," he said. "If you had come in the house with
them . . ." His voice trailed off. "They would have hurt her"—he
jerked his head toward me— "and then killed you both." Jeremy
looked happier. "Look," said the fat cop kindly, "there's no right or
wrong in the situation. There's just luck." He arranged to get Jeremy to
the hospital, and I sat there and waited for the horror of it all to overcome me.

All night I replayed the moment those black gloves came up 9
against the car window, and I saw, over and over, the ugly snout of the
gun peering greedily in at me. I wondered why I had felt so calm. I
had not been afraid—ever. I was hardly even there. All night the loop
of the gloves and the gun and the voice replayed itself in my mind, and
I waited for the right emotions to come and claim me.

How long did the whole thing last? Three minutes, five, eight? 10
How many hours of my life will I spend reliving it? Knowing that no

matter how many I do, there is no way to prepare for the next time, no intelligent response to a gun. The fat cop was right: There's only luck. The next time I might end up dead.

   And there will be a next time—I'm sure of that now. It can happen   11
anywhere, anytime, to anyone. Security is an illusion; there is no safety in locks or in numbers—or in guns. Guns make some people feel safe and some people feel strong, but they're fooling themselves.

Growing Up in the Shadow of an Older Brother or Sister

SALLY HELGESEN

Being the oldest child in a family is coming into the world *tabula* 1
rasa, with a clean slate; there is no model, no outline, no course one is
expected to follow. Being the oldest is being a pioneer who must explore and tame unchartered territories so that settlers who come afterward may find life better-defined, more secure. "I always felt I was
born old, born *knowing*, the youngest of five once told me, explaining
that she had witnessed enough mistakes by her older siblings to know
just what to avoid.

I felt envious. As the oldest of five, I always felt as if I'd been born 2
young, born *not* knowing. Nobody made my mistakes for me. The advantages of having an older brother or sister have always been apparent to me, but it wasn't until recently that I began to understand that
this particular blessing could be a mixed one, like most good things in
life.

The influence of an older child in the family may be so strong that 3
a younger spends a lifetime trying either to escape it or to live up to
imagined expectations. Although it's rare to encounter an older child
who's been profoundly influenced by a younger's opinion, it's common
to find those who, even in their forties and fifties, are still enslaved by
the opinions of a sibling only a year or two older. A younger child may
learn from an elder's blunders, but often pays for the knowledge with a
loss of freedom.

Let's listen again to that youngest child of five, the eighteen-year- 4
old who says she was born knowing, born old. "My brother is three
years older, and he had the most influence over me," she says. "He had
three older sisters, so when I came along he tried to make me into a
little brother. If I played with dolls, he laughed at me, so I tried to be
good at what he respected—mainly sports. He had a crush on a girl in
his class, Jody, who was a tomboy. She was my idol, too, so whenever he
thought I wasn't trying hard enough to win, he'd yell and say, *Don't you
want to be like her?* If I got hurt, he'd make me get up and keep my

mouth shut. Because of him, I learned to take pain and not cry. I'm glad of that—most girls seem like crybabies to me—but he also taught me that I had to stifle my feelings, so I learned to keep my emotions a secret. Sometimes I feel like I'm part guy because I understand so well how guys think. That makes me feel isolated from other kids. I can't imagine what I'd be like if I hadn't had a brother."

I can't imagine what I'd be like—how often younger children say that when referring to the influence of an older! And indeed, it's hard for me to imagine my friend without that peculiar code of toughness that she adopted under her brother's tutelage. Another young woman I know—recently married and still living in her small hometown—spoke of a similar inability to conceive of herself without her two older sisters.

"My whole world view was shaped by them," she said. "For one thing, both of them moved away from town when they were eighteen, so I always assumed that's what people should do. I've never wanted to leave town, but I feel like a failure because I haven't. My husband can't understand.

"When I first learned to walk, my sisters stood me in the middle and made me come to whomever I liked best. I guess I've always felt torn between them. The oldest one grew up before the hippie era; she was popular, wore pleated skirts and matching sweaters, and went to all the dances and football games. I just assumed I'd be like that, but when I got into high school, everyone was a hippie, and what I'd taken for granted didn't happen. My second sister had been a hippie—she sat in her room all day, writing poetry and listening to Bob Dylan. So again, I felt as though I had to choose between my sisters. The choice was a conflict, and I didn't realize there could be a way in between, just for myself."

Prompted by her second sister, this young woman rushed into sexual relationships before she felt ready or even wanted to have them, in order to win approval. I mention this because in talking to younger brothers and sisters, I found that older children exert a surprising influence upon younger ones in regard to sex. But although this is quite common, it's rarely talked about, so people feel peculiar in their experience, and resent it. Girls seem particularly influenced by older brothers.

One high-school girl described it this way: "When my brother started tenth grade, I was afraid he wouldn't hang around with me anymore because he began to like girls. But he spent more time with me than ever. Mostly, he'd talked about sex—what guys liked, what made them feel good. I felt self-conscious at school, because I knew so much more than the other kids. I felt older than them, so I started having sex younger. Sometimes I blame it on my brother, that my innocence was spoiled."

This girl might be much comforted if she were to learn how com- 10 mon her experience is. She might resent her brother less. Youngest children usually grow up fast—often faster than they would like to. They learn lessons simply because older children are eager to teach them. Parents seem unable to stop this; often, they're oblivious to what's going on. But, while the lessons younger children learn may propel them into a life for which they don't feel ready, the insights they gain by watching older kids at close range usually prepare them for more than they realize. Big brothers and sisters are, as I said, a mixed blessing. They may map out your path instead of allowing you to follow your own inclinations, but you can use their experience to move down that path more directly.

The Story of an Hour

KATE CHOPIN

Knowing that Mrs. Mallard was afflicted with a heart trouble, 1
great care was taken to break to her as gently as possible the news of
her husband's death.

It was her sister Josephine who told her, in broken sentences, 2
veiled hints that revealed in half concealing. Her husband's friend
Richards was there, too, near her. It was he who had been in the newspaper office when intelligence of the railroad disaster was received,
with Brently Mallard's name leading the list of "killed." He had only
taken the time to assure himself of its truth by a second telegram, and
had hastened to forestall any less careful, less tender friend in bearing
the sad message.

She did not hear the story as many women have heard the same, 3
with a paralyzed inability to accept its significance. She wept at once,
with sudden, wild abandonment, in her sister's arms. When the storm
of grief had spent itself she went to her room alone. She would have no
one follow her.

There stood, facing the open window, a comfortable, roomy arm- 4
chair. Into this she sank, pressed down by a physical exhaustion that
haunted her body and seemed to reach into her soul.

She could see in the open square before her house the tops of trees 5
that were all aquiver with the new spring life. The delicious breath of
rain was in the air. In the street below a peddler was crying his wares.
The notes of a distant song which some one was singing reached her
faintly, and countless sparrows were twittering in the eaves.

There were patches of blue sky showing here and there through 6
the clouds that had met and piled above the other in the west facing
her window.

She sat with her head thrown back upon the cushion of the chair 7
quite motionless, except when a sob came up into her throat and shook
her, as a child who has cried itself to sleep continues to sob in its
dreams.

She was young, with a fair, calm face, whose lines bespoke repres- 8
sion and even a certain strength. But now there was a dull stare in her

eyes, whose gaze was fixed away off yonder on one of those patches of blue sky. It was not a glance of reflection, but rather indicated a suspension of intelligent thought.

There was something coming to her and she was waiting for it, 9 fearfully. What was it? She did not know; it was too subtle and elusive to name. But she felt it, creeping out of the sky, reaching toward her through the sounds, the scents, the color that filled the air.

Now her bosom rose and fell tumultuously. She was beginning to 10 recognize this thing that was approaching to possess her, and she was striving to beat it back with her will—as powerless as her two white slender hands would have been.

When she abandoned herself a little whispered word escaped her 11 slightly parted lips. She said it over and over under her breath: "Free, free, free!" The vacant stare and the look of terror that had followed it went from her eyes. They stayed keen and bright. Her pulses beat fast, and the coursing blood warmed and relaxed every inch of her body.

She did not stop to ask if it were not a monstrous joy that held her. 12 A clear and exalted perception enabled her to dismiss the suggestion as trivial.

She knew that she would weep again when she saw the kind, tender 13 hands folded in death; the face that had never looked save with love upon her, fixed and gray and dead. But she saw beyond that bitter moment a long procession of years to come that would belong to her absolutely. And she opened and spread her arms out to them in welcome.

There would be no one to live for during those coming years; she 14 would live for herself. There would be no powerful will bending her in that blind persistence with which men and women believe they have a right to impose a private will upon a fellow-creature. A kind intention or a cruel intention made the act seem no less a crime as she looked upon it in that brief moment of illumination.

And yet she had loved him—sometimes. Often she had not. What 15 did it matter! What could love, the unsolved mystery, count for in face of this possession of self-assertion which she suddenly recognized as the strongest impulse of her being!

"Free! Body and soul free!" she kept whispering. 16

Josephine was kneeling before the closed door with her lips to the 17 keyhole, imploring for admission. "Louise, open the door! I beg; open the door—you will make yourself ill. What are you doing, Louise? For heaven's sake open the door."

"Go away. I am not making myself ill." No; she was drinking in a 18 very elixir of life through that open window.

Her fancy was running riot along those days ahead of her. Spring 19 days, and summer days, and all sorts of days that would be her own.

She breathed a quick prayer that life might be long. It was only yester-
day she had thought with a shudder that life might be long.

She arose at length and opened the door to her sister's impor- 20
tunities. There was a feverish triumph in her eyes, and she carried
herself unwittingly like a goddess of Victory. She clasped her sister's
waist, and together they descended the stairs. Richards stood waiting
for them at the bottom.

Some one was opening the front door with a latchkey. It was 21
Brently Mallard who entered, a little travel-stained, composedly carry-
ing his grip-sack and umbrella. He had been far from the scene of
accident, and did not even know there had been one. He stood amazed
at Josephine's piercing cry; at Richards's quick motion to screen him
from the view of his wife.

But Richards was too late.   22

When the doctors came they said she had died of heart disease—of 23
joy that kills.

PART THREE

Responding to Ideas

In Part Three the readings focus especially on ideas and are likely to trigger your own ideas in response. Although all reading and writing involve ideas in one way or another, the essays and stories in this part explore particular ideas that interested the authors. These readings, then, are like your own essays: The authors chose a topic and developed lines of argument and examples to support their ideas. The authors take a stand and express themselves, just as you have been doing in your essays for Parts One and Two.

When writing about ideas, it is especially important to select and limit your topic carefully and to organize your supporting examples and details to good effect. Whether you simply want to express your ideas or want to persuade your readers to accept your point of view, by sharing your work with classmates and friends you can learn whether your ideas are clear and convincing.

In responding to the readings that follow, remember that the goal is to discover your own ideas—not necessarily those which might be popular with your classmates or acceptable to your instructor. If you identify ideas that are important to you, you should be able to present them in an interesting, persuasive manner.

Intelligence

ISAAC ASIMOV

What is intelligence, anyway? When I was in the army I re- 1
ceived a kind of aptitude test that all soldiers took and, against a normal of 100, scored 160. No one at the base had ever seen a figure like
that, and for two hours they made a big fuss over me. (It didn't mean
anything. The next day I was still a buck private with KP as my highest
duty.)

All my life I've been registering scores like that, so that I have the 2
complacent feeling that I'm highly intelligent, and I expect other people to think so, too. Actually, though, don't such scores simply mean
that I am very good at answering the type of academic questions that
are considered worthy of answers by the people who make up the intelligence tests—people with intellectual bents similar to mine?

For instance, I had an auto-repair man once, who, on these intel- 3
ligence tests, could not possibly have scored more than 80, by my esti-
mate. I always took it for granted that I was far more intelligent than
he was. Yet, when anything went wrong with my car I hastened to him
with it, watched him anxiously as he explored its vitals, and listened to
his pronouncements as though they were divine oracles—and he always fixed my car.

Well, then, suppose my auto-repair man devised questions for an 4
intelligence test. Or suppose a carpenter did, or a farmer, or, indeed,
almost anyone but an academician. By every one of those tests, I'd
prove myself a moron. And I'd *be* a moron, too. In a world where I
could not use my academic training and my verbal talents but had to do
something intricate or hard, working with my hands, I would do
poorly. My intelligence, then, is not absolute but is a function of the
society I live in and of the fact that a small subsection of that society has
managed to foist itself on the rest as an arbiter of such matters.

Consider my auto-repair man, again. He had a habit of telling me 5
jokes whenever he saw me. One time he raised his head from under
the automobile hood to say: "Doc, a deaf-and-dumb guy went into a
hardware store to ask for some nails. He put two fingers together on

the counter and made hammering motions with the other hand. The clerk brought him a hammer. He shook his head and pointed to the two fingers he was hammering. The clerk brought him nails. He picked out the sizes he wanted, and left. Well, doc, the next guy who came in was a blind man. He wanted scissors. How do you suppose he asked for them?"

Indulgently, I lifted my right hand and made scissoring motions   6
with my first two fingers. Whereupon my auto-repair man laughed raucously and said, "Why, you dumb jerk, he used his *voice* and asked for them." Then he said, smugly, "I've been trying that on all my customers today." "Did you catch many?" I asked. "Quite a few," he said, "but I knew for sure I'd catch *you*." "Why is that?" I asked. "Because you're so goddamned educated, doc, I *knew* you couldn't be very smart."

And I have an uneasy feeling he had something there.   7

SAMPLE RESPONSES to "Intelligence"

Responder 1: Alex ─────────────────────────

Right on! This writer said what I've been saying for a long time, but he said it better. This whole society is going nuts over putting people in school and keeping them there. They think that because a person reads some books and swallows information about different subjects, that person is going to be intelligent. No way! Book learning is okay for some people, but other people are smart in different ways. Like Asimov told us--his auto repairman was a genius at fixing cars, but he probably couldn't score 80 on an intelligence test. I have friends who are going to college and friends who aren't. Some of the friends who aren't going are, in my opinion, smarter than the ones who are going. So what am I doing in college? I made a deal with my father. He

said, "Go for a year, and if you don't like it, you can
quit and work full time." I think he was sure I was going
to like it. But I don't. In fact, I'm dropping out (how
horrible!) after this semester. This essay was the only
interesting thing I've read since I've been here.

Responder 2: Jerry ─────────────────────────────

It's nice when somebody's so successful he can
pretend that he's not so great. Isaac Asimov is a famous
and rich writer. He's written a lot of science-fiction
books and even factual books about science. I've read
two or three of his science-fiction books, and I enjoyed
them. So I'm not saying Asimov isn't a good writer,
because he is. What I'm saying is that knows he's very
intelligent and successful, and so he can make fun of
himself without worrying that anybody will take him
seriously. Oh, yeah, he can say his mechanic is smart
when it comes to fixing cars. But so what? The mechanic
will be a working stiff all his life, and he'll never
have a small fraction of the money that Asimov has.
Asimov probably makes more money from one of his books
than most people make in their lifetimes. Why should he
worry about having his car fixed? He could buy a new car
every month if he wanted to. I wish people wouldn't be so
phony. Don't you love it when rich people, like famous
movie or TV stars, tell us that money isn't everything.
For them it isn't, because they've got plenty. It's nice
for Asimov to say that his intelligence isn't any better

than his mechanic's. Oh, sure, it isn't. It's only a
million dollars better.

Responder 3: Millie

In high school there was a girl I have to describe as
a real genius. She was a wiz in every subject. The math
teacher even admitted that Phyllis (that was her name)
knew more than he did.

But talk about sick. I mean that girl was the
weirdest kid in school. She had no friends, even though
some of us tried to be friendly with her. I asked her if
she would like to eat lunch with me. I figured she really
wanted a friend but was too shy. You know, she never even
said anything. Just shook her head and walked away. And
she wasn't bad looking. A couple of boys asked her if she
would like to go out sometime. She told them she wasn't
interested in going out because she had other things to
do. One of the boys told me she was the coldest fish he
ever talked to.

So I guess Phyllis was smart, but if being smart
makes you so weird, you can have it. I'd rather be just
average in intelligence but also a human being.

Responder 4: Jean

Society decides how valuable something is. That's
why a smart auto mechanic doesn't get as much respect as
a doctor or a lawyer. People may respect a mechanic's

skill at fixing things, but nobody invites him on television to give his opinions about what's going on in the world. Maybe a mechanic has the intelligence to solve some of the problems in our society. However, we'll never hear his opinions, because no one will ever ask him.

I think we kid ourselves when we talk about all the opportunities in our country. Most of the important positions are filled by people who come from the "right" families and go to the "best" schools. Two people may have a college degree. However, a degree from a prestigious college is worth more than a degree from an ordinary college. Things aren't equal, because some people are born with a head start over the rest of us. We can all dream about reaching the top, but very few of us will be able to crack the system that the ruling class has set up for its own benefit.

CONSIDERING THE RESPONSES

Response 1: Alex

Apparently, Alex doesn't value a college degree very highly. He claims that some of his noncollege friends are smarter than his college friends. Furthermore, he questions society's emphasis on education or, at least, on schooling. He seems to have gotten little from his classes so far, and he expresses his intention to drop out and go to work full time. Based on his response, do you think Alex can write a convincing essay on the idea that a college education isn't needed by everyone in our society? What problems do you see in planning an essay which might convince us that his observation is reasonable?

Response 2: Jerry ——————————————————————

Jerry thinks that successful people are so secure that they can play down their talents. He sees a streak of phoniness in Asimov's praise for his auto mechanic's intelligence, as well as in the pronouncements of rich people who tell us that money isn't everything. In fact, Jerry seems to equate intelligence with the ability to make money. Do you think an essay can be written defending the ideas in Jerry's response? Why or why not? Would an essay that argues against Jerry's ideas be easier to write?

Response 3: Millie ——————————————————————

Millie's experiences with Phyllis lead her to suggest that highly intelligent people have problems fitting in socially. Millie calls Phyllis "the weirdest kid in school," a judgment which later leads her to imply that—when it comes to being a human being—her own "average" intelligence is preferable to Phyllis's "genius." Do you think Millie can support her idea that high intelligence leads to social maladjustment? Why or why not? If Millie wants to write about Phyllis, what topic sentence or controlling idea might she use to guide her essay?

Response 4: Jean ——————————————————————

Jean's response contains several ideas that might be developed into an interesting essay. Does the idea that a person's profession may *automatically* confer respect and status seem like a promising topic? Why or why not? What difficulties do you foresee in planning such an essay? In Jean's opinion, a degree from one of the "best" schools is more valuable than a degree from "an ordinary college." How might this line of reasoning be pursued in an essay?

No Allusions in the Classroom

JAIME M. O'NEILL

Josh Billings, a 19th-century humorist, wrote that it is better "not 1
to know so much than to know so many things that ain't so." Recently,
after 15 years of teaching in community colleges, I decided to take a
sampling to find out what my students know that ain't so. I did this out
of a growing awareness that they don't always understand what I say. I
suspected that part of their failure to understand derived from the fact
that they did not catch my allusions. An allusion to a writer, a geo-
graphical locality or a historical episode inevitably produced telltale ex-
pressions of bewilderment.

There is a game played by students and teachers everywhere. The 2
game goes like this: the teacher tries to find out what students don't
know so that he can correct those deficiencies; the students, concerned
with grades and slippery self-images, try to hide their ignorance in every way they can. So it is that students seldom ask pertinent questions.
So it is that teachers assume that students possess basic knowledge
which, in fact, they don't possess.

Last semester I broke the rules of this time-honored game when I 3
presented my English-composition students with an 86-question "general knowledge" test on the first day of class. There were 26 people in
the class; they ranged in age from 18 to 54. They had all completed at
least one quarter of college-level work.

Here is a sampling of what they knew that just ain't so: 4

Creative

Ralph Nader is a baseball player. Charles Darwin invented gravity. 5
Christ was born in the 16th century. J. Edgar Hoover was a 19th-cen-
tury president. Neil Simon wrote "One Flew Over the Cuckoo's Nest";
"The Great Gatsby" was a magician in the 1930s. Franz Joseph Haydn
was a songwriter during the same decade. Sid Caesar was an early Ro-
man emperor. Mark Twain invented the cotton gin. Heinrich Himmler
invented the Heimlich maneuver. Jefferson Davis was a guitar player
for The Jefferson Airplane. Benito Mussolini was a Russian leader of
the 18th century; Dwight D. Eisenhower came earlier, serving as a

110

president during the 17th century. William Faulkner made his name as a 17th-century scientist. All of these people must have appreciated the work of Pablo Picasso, who painted masterpieces in the 12th century.

My students were equally creative in their understanding of geography. They knew, for instance, that Managua is the capital of Vietnam, that Cape Town is in the United States and that Beirut is in Germany. Bogotá, of course, is in Borneo (unless it is in China). Camp David is in Israel, and Stratford-on-Avon is in Grenada (or Gernada). Gdansk is in Ireland. Cologne is in the Virgin Islands. Mazatlán is in Switzerland. Belfast was variously located in Egypt, Germany, Belgium and Italy. Leningrad was transported to Jamaica; Montreal to Spain. 6

And on it went. Most students answered incorrectly far more often than they answered correctly. Several of them meticulously wrote "I don't know" 86 times, or 80 times, or 62 times. 7

They did not like the test. Although I made it clear that the test would not be graded, they did not like having their ignorance exposed. One of them dismissed the test by saying, "Oh, I get it; it's like Trivial Pursuit." Imagining a game of Trivial Pursuit among some of today's college students is a frightening thought; such a game could last for years. 8

But the comment bothered me. What, in this time in our global history, is trivial? And what is essential? Perhaps it no longer matters very much if large numbers of people in the world's oldest democratic republic know little of their own history and even less about the planet they inhabit. 9

But I expect that it does matter. I also suspect that my students provide a fairly good cross section of the general population. There are 1,274 two-year colleges in the United States that collectively enroll nearly 5 million students. I have taught at four of those colleges in two states, and I doubt that my questionnaire would have produced different results at any of them. My colleagues at universities tell me that they would not be surprised at similar undergraduate answers. 10

My small sampling is further corroborated by recent polls which disclosed that a significant number of American adults have no idea which side the United States supported in Vietnam and that a majority of the general populace have no idea which side the United States is currently supporting in Nicaragua or El Salvador. 11

Less importantly, a local marketing survey asked a sampling of young computer whizzes to identify the character in IBM's advertising campaign that is based on an allusion to Charlie Chaplin in "Modern Times." Few of them had heard of Charlie Chaplin, fewer heard or knew about the movie classic. 12

Common Heritage

As I write this, the radio is broadcasting the news about the Walker 13
family. Accused of spying for the Soviets, the Walkers, according to a
U.S. attorney, will be the Rosenbergs of the '80s. One of my students
thought Ethel Rosenberg was a singer from the 1930s. The rest of
them didn't know. Communication depends, to some extent, upon the
ability to make (and catch) allusions, to share a common understanding
and a common heritage. Even preliterate societies can claim this shared
assessment of their world. As we enter the postindustrial "information
processing" age, what sort of information will be processed? And, as
the educational establishment is driven "back to the basics," isn't it time
we decided that a common understanding of our history and our
planet is most basic of all?

As a teacher, I find myself in the ignorance-and-hope business. 14
Each year hopeful faces confront me, trying to conceal their ignorance.
Their hopes ride on the dispelling of that ignorance.

All our hopes do.   15

We should begin servicing that hope more responsibly and dispell- 16
ing that ignorance with a more systematic approach to imparting essential knowledge.

Socrates, the American Indian chieftain, would have wanted it that 17
way.

SAMPLE RESPONSES to "No Allusions in the Classroom"

Responder 1: Gary ————————————————————

Why do teachers think everything they know is so

important? And why does this one believe the answers

that the students gave to his questions? I know I'd give

a flip answer if I wasn't sure what the test was all

about.

Who'd feel stupid if he didn't know the name of some

old comedian on early television or a Nazi police

officer who's been dead forty years? This teacher lived

back in those days, and so he remembers it all from the

movies and the news when he was growing up. We'll remember Son of Sam and Steve Martin, but our grandchildren won't have any idea who they were. I won't expect them to, either, but then I'm not a teacher.

And geography! That's like knowing the names of all the stars and the constellations. I bet he wouldn't know Sirius is the nearest star (Oops, I forgot the sun) or what the Pleiades look like. And he'd never guess what Dragon Slayer is.

If he's going to publish all those wrong answers before a national audience, then no wonder so many of the students answered "no comment." I sure wouldn't want to be in his class. But I'm afraid I've got a couple of teachers just like him this semester.

Responder 2: Gwen

I can't believe anybody in college doesn't know most of the things on this teacher's questionnaire. Nobody could be expected to know them all, but everybody should know some of them, like Jesus, Darwin, and Socrates. I guess some people find it hard to remember for very long the things they learn for tests. Maybe they have to keep hearing about someone or some place for it to stick in their minds. Maybe he should have given them multiple choices to jog their memories. Then he wouldn't have gotten wild guesses. But still, we forget so much because there is so much we are expected to learn, and it's hard to tell what's really important.

Even his test might confuse someone from another
country. They might think all the names and places are
very important. But Neil Simon, William Faulkner,
Cologne, and Bogota are not nearly as significant as
Beirut, Eisenhower, Mark Twain, and Picasso. And some
names might be recognizable if they came up in our
reading, where our attention would be pointed in the
right direction by the topic. Also, if I wasn't sure how
to spell Beirut, I might have been fooled. Some people
are truly ignorant, and they won't last long in college
unless they learn an awful lot and very fast. But I think
the test doesn't mean all that much.

Responder 3: Yvette

I thought I came to college to learn, but this man
thinks I should know everything right now. I was
encouraged to return to school now that my family are
all in their teens or married. My son is also going to
college, but not this one. But if I had been tested like
this on the first day, I'd have quit right then and
there. I'm supposed to know all these names? Actually I
did know some of the ones that he put on the test just to
show he isn't a snob (Neil Simon and Sid Caesar). I
suppose the list of things the students didn't know is
full of answers that would seem humorous if I knew who
the people and places really are. But I didn't know most
of them. And I don't think it is funny that someone
didn't know when Christ lived. Maybe he was Jewish or a

Hindu. I've forgotten some things he says I should know,
like whose side we were on in the Vietnam War. I only
know we were on the wrong side, since they lost. Also,
I'm a little confused by his last quotation. I thought
Socrates was the name of an ancient Greek philosopher.
If it is also an Indian chief, history is going to be
much harder than I expected.

CONSIDERING THE RESPONSES

Response 1: Gary

Gary felt at a loss for a topic. He realized that just criticizing the test questions one by one would not result in an "essay," but he couldn't see how his objections to this teacher's approach could be turned into a topic that would interest anyone. What do you think is the main idea in Gary's response? Does any sentence in his response sum up that idea? What topic sentence would you advise Gary to use in focusing his ideas? What kinds of examples should he use to develop his main idea? Will those examples prove his point, or does he need to go beyond his own observations?

Response 2: Gwen

Gwen's response revealed mixed feelings about this essay. She tended to agree that students should be better informed, but she also made excuses for their poor performance on this questionnaire. Should Gwen develop a paper about poorly designed tests or about poorly prepared students? Which topic is a better response to O'Neill's essay? Why?

Response 3: Yvette

Yvette was intimidated by Professor O'Neill's questionnaire, because she is not as well informed as she would like to be. In fact, most of her response is about why she herself would do poorly on this test. What do you think Yvette should write about? Is her response about the essay or about herself? What topic sentence should she explore? Depending on your answer, how should Yvette develop her essay? What ideas and examples should she offer, and how should she organize them?

What Makes Some Things Wrong?

HAROLD KUSHNER

A rabbi is a teacher. I teach in many ways, formally and informally, by precept and by example. Some years ago, I taught a class in modern Jewish history for teenagers in my congregation. We spent a lot of time on the Holocaust, the destruction of six million Jewish men, women, and children at the hands of the Nazis because they were Jews. As we read example after example of sadism, butchery, and cruelty, I could see the cumulative outrage in the souls of my students reaching the boiling point. They were so angry at what had been done to helpless victims not long before they were born, in some cases in countries where they might well have lived if their grandparents had not left Europe for America.

When we were done studying this history of those years, I asked them, "Why was Hitler wrong?"

They were confused by my question. "What do you mean, why was Hitler wrong?" one student asked incredulously. "Do you mean he may have been right that the Jews were an inferior race and should be murdered?"

Another cried, "Why was he wrong? You can't just take people and kill them because you don't like them!"

"Remember," I pointed out to them, "the Nazis were careful to pass laws sanctioning everything they did. It was all within the law. Was it still wrong?"

"Well, of course it was," the first student replied. "You can't pass laws permitting the gassing of little children just because they're Jewish."

"Are you trying to tell me that some things are wrong even if a majority of the people think they are right? Are you telling me that there is such a thing as right and wrong built into the human conscience, and it's not just a matter of how you feel about it?"

Again they looked confused, and one finally answered, "Well, yeah, I guess so. I never thought about it that way before."

SAMPLE RESPONSES to "What Makes Some Things Wrong?"

Responder 1: Alfred ⸺⸺⸺⸺⸺⸺⸺⸺

Human beings make laws. Sometimes the laws they make are bad, even if a majority of the people go along with them. Even in this country, which is a democracy, we have passed some laws that were wrong. We once had laws that said people could own slaves. Did you ever hear of anything more ridiculous! But in a democracy, bad laws will be changed. People can protest. People can speak out. People can vote. Under crazy Hitler and the Nazis, once a law was passed, there was no way to change it, even if the people wanted to.

The German people went along with Hitler's insanity, and this caused millions of innocent people to be murdered. This shows you what can happen when insanity and evil win out over goodness.

Responder 2: Isabel ⸺⸺⸺⸺⸺⸺⸺⸺

Kushner raises a very controversial issue when he talks about right and wrong being "built into the human conscience." If he means that we are born with a knowledge of right and wrong, then I'm not sure I would agree with him as easily as his students seem to have agreed with him. Yes, I believe that it's wrong to kill people just because you don't like their race, or religion, or their customs. But I wasn't born with this belief. It was taught to me over many years at home, in my church, and in school. In other words, my conscience developed as I grew up in my environment. Also, people in different cultures feel differently about certain actions. For example, in my religion it is considered a grave sin to commit suicide. Even if my whole life fell apart and I saw no purpose in living, I would not kill myself because my conscience would not allow me to. However, I know that in some areas of the world, where people have different customs and different religions, committing suicide is not considered a sin. A person who decides to kill himself in one of those cultures would not be stopped by his conscience.

We learn right from wrong from things that influence us in our culture and society. It would be nice to believe that we are born with a built-in sense of good and evil, but I doubt that this is the case.

Responder 3: Paul

The author is right. These days many people think they can decide about what's right and what's wrong based on how they "feel" about what they do or what's going on around them. These people are confused. Some things are right and some things are wrong, and it doesn't matter how a person feels about them.

When God gave us the Ten Commandments, He didn't say that we could follow the ones we feel like following and

ignore the ones we don't feel like following. No, we
have to follow all of them because God decides what's
good and what's evil in this world. If everybody in the
country voted to make murder legal, it would still be
wrong to kill people. Human beings don't decide on the
rules for good behavior. God does. And God said, "Thou
shalt not kill." That's all there is to it.

Responder 4: Elliot

If we're all supposed to have consciences that tell
us right from wrong, then how come so many people in the
world don't seem to be bothered by them? If we say that
all people like to eat or need to eat, then there's no
argument. You can just look around and see that the
statement is true because everybody will eat, so long as
there is food around. But if you say everybody has a
conscience that tells them right from wrong, and then
you look around and see an awful lot of people who don't
seem to know right from wrong, I have to wonder. So I
don't know about this built in conscience business. I'll
have to think about that one for a while.

CONSIDERING THE RESPONSES

Responder 1: Alfred

Alfred agrees with Kushner's contention that a law can be wrong
even if a majority of people are in favor of it. Alfred says that unjust
laws can be passed even in a democracy. However, according to
Alfred, unjust laws will be changed in a democracy, while unjust laws,

once agreed upon, cannot be changed in a dictatorship. What assumption does Alfred make about people in a democracy when he says that bad laws will be changed under a democratic system? Would he be able to support such an assumption by giving a number of examples of unjust laws that were changed because they proved to be unjust to certain groups in our country? Can you offer Alfred examples of unjust laws that are still a part of our country's system? If Alfred agrees with you about the unjustness of one or more of these laws, how would he be able to explain their existence while still maintaining his faith in democracy?

Responder 2: Isabel

In her response, Isabel refers to suicide in different cultures as an example of how conscience can develop differently in different societies. Does this example prove her point? Would she need other examples to convince readers that people develop conscience from their relationship to the culture in which they live? Could Isabel write an essay in which she explains, in detail, how she came to hold a particular belief about a controversial issue that many people disagree about today? What kind of details would she need to include in her essay?

Responder 3: Paul

In discussing Paul's response, several students questioned whether the Ten Commandments actually covered all the situations in which people might have trouble distinguishing right from wrong. Do you think Paul would be able to answer the kinds of questions made by the students while still supporting his belief that God has provided us with a code that clearly tells us how to behave? Would Paul have to expand his explanation of God's rules in order to answer these questions? How might he do so in an essay?

Responder 4: Elliot

Elliot has doubts about Kushner's belief that knowing right and wrong is built into the human conscience. Does Elliot's contrast between the obvious human desire to eat and not-so-obvious desire to do good make for a valid objection to Kushner's belief? Could Elliot expand this contrast into a full essay that argues against a built-in sense of right and wrong? How could Elliot support his suggestion that conscience does not seem to bother many people in the world?

Reflections on a Hockey Helmet

GREGORY BAYAN

I was in the middle of a hockey game recently when I overheard 1
two young spectators arguing about the way I play. I heard the words
"very brave" and "very foolish," attributes I would never use to describe myself. Yet every year at this time I am besieged by ever-increas-
ing numbers of well-meaning people who suggest or plead that I cease
my sacrilege and start to play it safe. The cause of this concern is simple: I refuse to wear a protective helmet.

This expression of individuality does not come cheaply or frivo- 2
lously. Bareheaded ice-hockey players are banned from all officially
sanctioned amateur play, including school, college, junior and interna-
tional competition. I am forever banished to the netherworld of semi-
private club hockey in men's amateur leagues, the only refuge where
my vanishing species is still allowed to exist.

The decision not to wear a helmet involves intensely personal feel- 3
ings that transcend safety. I find the helmet to be physically uncomfortable, but more important, it strikes me as being anti-individual and
esthetically repellent. Look at film clips of the 1960 U.S. Olympic
hockey team's gold-medal victory at Squaw Valley, when not even the
Russians wore helmets. Now watch a clip of any of this year's hockey
matches, where helmets are mandatory. There's something missing.
The human element of daring independence is gone. As much as I
love the sport, I can no longer watch televised hockey. I simply cannot
relate to the players as human beings when they all resemble identical
automatons.

Like a dorsal fin that breaks water and heralds the presence of a 4
leviathan, so the helmet is a metaphor for something deeply wrong in
America.

Protection

Helmets are a sign we've entered the era of the Hardhead. A 5
Hardhead is one who seeks to protect us not only from others, but
from ourselves. He is creating a Huxley-like world where all irritating
incongruities among individuals are being conveniently erased in the

122

name of safety. Americans are afraid, afraid of risk. We want absolute personal safety, and we want it guaranteed and mandatory.

Perhaps it's because we now enjoy such an unprecedented degree 6 of safety, compared with the past, that previously disregarded risks stand out in such bold relief. The great population destroyers of rampant disease, impure food and unduly hazardous working conditions have been largely brought under control, reducing the average person's daily contact with death and injury to a level thought impossible only a few decades ago. This is obviously a good thing. I shed no tears for smallpox and polio. I feel better having the Food and Drug Administration monitor the presence of rodent hairs in my frozen pizza, rather than being forced to take up a microscope and do the job myself. Government should try to protect its citizens from external malice and negligence beyond the individual's control, but there is a fine line between necessary protection and unwarranted interferences.

When the Hardheads go to work on dismantling freedom of 7 choice, that's when I put my skate down. When the phrase *it's for your own good* determines every direction of personal initiative, then I know we've embraced the philosophy of the Pringle's potato chip—uniformity and monotony. Domed sports stadiums are springing up like mushrooms to protect us from the unpredictable. Speedometers read no faster than 85 mph to protect us from the temptations of curiosity. U.S. amateur boxers must now wear headgear for their own good. Our automobiles now buzz us to buckle up for our own good. CBS is even taking the scissors to The Bugs Bunny/Road Runner cartoon show, lest scenes of excessive "violence" feed our latent homicidal impulses. All for our own good.

America is being smothered by safety. Sometimes I think if Henry 8 Hudson were to suddenly reappear in New York Bay, he would be arrested and placed under observation, and the leaky old Half Moon would be impounded for innumerable construction violations.

There is no such thing as complete safety. When Astroturf first 9 came out, its uniform surface was touted as a way to reduce injury. There now exists an entire lexicon of Astro-turf-induced injuries, such as "Astro-burn" and "Astro-knee." There are examples of people who have been thrown from their cars and spared from death in terrible accidents because they were *not* wearing their seat belts. Motorcycle helmets have been known to cause whiplash. Government statistics tell us that the leading cause of personal injury in the United States is people falling down—in bathtubs, on stairs, off ladders, everywhere. Despite our best efforts to the contrary, the universe still appears to be firmly in the grip of Murphy's Law (if something can go wrong, it will).

Mandatory armor, worn at all times, and a life spent huddled in a 10 bomb shelter may result in longevity—but what kind of life is that? To those who demand an utterly protected and predictable existence I say fine, good luck, but don't include me in your mandate.

Maverick

Freedom of choice is the only thing that separates the living from 11
the dead. We need it, with all of its inherent dangers. We need the risk taker, the maverick, the thorn in the side of conformity. We need Martin Luther, John Lennon, George Willig, Sir Thomas More, Jack Paar and Wile E. Coyote. And ice hockey's Hobey Baker. We need every last bit of individuality we can get. Without it, life loses the glorious zest of freedom and diversity, of fantasy and change.

Which brings me back to the helmet. I would never impose my 12
personal preference on others. All I claim is the same consideration for myself.

I realize the risk involved in the simple act of playing ice hockey 13
without wearing a helmet, and I accept it, the same as I accept the fact that I won't live forever. When the Hardheads change that fact, when they finally succeed in loading life's dice, that's when I'll hang up my skates.

For my own good.   14

SAMPLE RESPONSES to "Reflections on a Hockey Helmet"

Responder 1: Sheila ————————————————————

I feel that this writer goes much too far. He isn't really talking about hockey helmets. He is against all government safety rules, even some of the ones he says are not so bad. He doesn't want seatbelts or a 55-mph speed limit on highways. It's jerks like him who cause trouble for the rest of us. When someone is injured badly in a car accident, our insurance premiums have to go up to pay for the medical bills. The 55-mph speed limit and mandatory seatbelt laws reduce the number of those accidents, and that's good for everybody. I also think the writer's wife would be very angry if he were paralyzed after hitting his head on the ice and then she had to feed and do everything else for him all the rest of her life.

Responder 2: Stan

This guy is all right in my book. The government tells us motorcycle clubbers we can't ride without a helmet, too. That's pure BS. A bunch of us drove to Massachusetts and protested this stupid law. There were girls in our gang, too. They won't wear helmets either, because they like feeling their hair blowin' in the wind when we hit the open road. If you're going to get killed, you'll get it one way or the other. They have no right to fine us for not obeying their stupid rules. Besides, it's just their way of harassing us bikers. They don't stop car drivers who don't wear seatbelts, but they never miss sticking it to us.

Responder 3: Anwar

Well, this writer has raised an interesting issue. It has to do with individual freedom versus the tendency of society to impose certain rules of behavior that it wants all people to follow. On the one hand, some people want to be free to follow their desires and preferences, no matter what society says. On the other hand, society believes it has the right to protect individuals from

doing harm to themselves and to others. Society, of
course, cannot allow people to be individualistic in all
ways. There must be some limits put on actions that
conflict with the beliefs and preferences of the
majority of the citizens. If some people cannot conform
in a reasonable manner, they must be restricted or
punished. Civilization must be preserved for the
majority.

Responder 4: Melina _____

I don't know from hockey helmets. I guess I would
say that this character is being stupid and stubborn.
We're all going to die soon enough, so why tempt fate?
But in some ways I know what he's talking about.
Sometimes I get mad when they try to stop me from doing
what I want to do. For instance, I'm a heavy smoker. I
don't know why but I am. And anytime I'm in a place with
"no smoking" signs, the first thing I look for is some
corner where I can have a cigarette. I don't know why,
but those "no smoking" signs make me mad.

CONSIDERING THE RESPONSES

Responder 1: Sheila _____

The class felt that Sheila could develop an interesting essay based
on her point that people who like to take risks "cause trouble for the
rest of us." Sheila gave one example of how auto accident injuries
affect the rest of us. She also speculated on the effect that a risk-

taker's injury can have on a loved one. Could Sheila expand and develop these two examples enough to constitute a full essay? Will she need other examples and explanations? What kind of plan for organizing an essay based on Sheila's idea can you suggest?

Responder 2: Stan

Four students in class agreed strongly with Stan's contention that law-enforcement officers go out of their way to "stick it to" motorcyclists. They urged Stan to write an essay exposing the police harassment that makes cyclists victims of an "unfair" law. Would Stan be able to write such an essay? What problems might he confront in attempting to do so? Do you see any other possible topics for writing that might grow out of Stan's response?

Responder 3: Anwar

Anwar's response led to a spirited discussion. One suggestion for Anwar was that he write an essay defending the right of society to protect reckless individuals from themselves. Another suggestion called on Anwar to explain how his belief in conforming to the will of the majority does not conflict with our ideals of individual freedom. Would the ideas in these two suggestions need to be discussed in order for Anwar to defend his beliefs? If not, how do the two suggestions differ? How would Anwar be able to defend his opinions if he chose to write about one or both of the suggested subjects?

Responder 4: Melina

Melina's response brought out a number of questions that might lead to possible essay topics. Why do people smoke when they know they are risking their health and perhaps their lives? Why does Melina get mad at no-smoking signs? Why does she feel the need to disobey such signs? Do most of us feel free to criticize other people's risk-taking while making up excuses for our own? From which of these questions do you think Melina could most easily derive a writing topic? Explain your answer.

How about Low-cost Drugs for Addicts?

LOUIS NIZER

We are losing the war against drug addiction. Our strategy is 1
wrong. I propose a different approach.

The Government should create clinics, manned by psychiatrists, 2
that would provide drugs for nominal charges or even free to addicts
under controlled regulations. It would cost the Government only 20
cents for a heroin shot, for which the addicts must now pay the mob
more than $100, and there are similar price discrepancies in cocaine,
crack and other such substances.

Such a service, which would also include the staff support of psy- 3
chiatrists and doctors, would cost a fraction of what the nation now
spends to maintain the land, sea and air apparatus necessary to inter-
dict illegal imports of drugs. There would also be a savings of hundreds of millions of dollars from the elimination of the prosecutorial
procedures that stifle our courts and overcrowd our prisons.

We see in our newspapers the triumphant announcements by Gov- 4
ernment agents that they have intercepted huge caches of cocaine, the
street prices of which are in the tens of millions of dollars. Should we
be gratified? Will this achievement reduce the number of addicts by
one? All it will do is increase the cost to the addict of his illegal supply.

Many addicts who are caught committing a crime admit that they 5
have mugged or stolen as many as six or seven times a day to accumu-
late the $100 needed for a fix. Since many of them need two or three

fixes a day, particularly for crack, one can understand the terror in our streets and homes. It is estimated that there are in New York City alone 200,000 addicts, and this is typical of cities across the nation. Even if we were to assume that only a modest percentage of a city's addicts engage in criminal conduct to obtain the money for the habit, requiring multiple muggings and thefts each day, we could nevertheless account for many of the tens of thousands of crimes each day in New York City alone.

Not long ago, a Justice Department division issued a report stating   6
that more than half the perpetrators of murder and other serious crimes were under the influence of drugs. This symbolizes the new domestic terror in our nation. This is why our citizens are unsafe in broad daylight on the most traveled thoroughfares. This is why typewriters and television sets are stolen from offices and homes and sold for a pittance. This is why parks are closed to the public and why murders are committed. This is why homes need multiple locks, and burglary systems, and why store windows, even in the most fashionable areas, require iron gates.

The benefits of the new strategy to control this terrorism would be   7
immediate and profound.

First, the mob would lose the main source of its income. It could   8
not compete against a free supply for which previously it exacted tribute estimated to be hundreds of millions of dollars, perhaps billions, from hopeless victims.

Second, pushers would be put out of business. There would be no   9
purpose in creating addicts who would be driven by desperate compulsion to steal and kill for the money necessary to maintain their habit. Children would not be enticed. The mob's macabre public-relations program is to tempt children with free drugs in order to create customers for the future. The wave of street crimes in broad daylight would diminish to a trickle. Homes and stores would not have to be fortresses. Our recreational areas could again be used. Neighborhoods would not be scandalized by sordid street centers where addicts gather to obtain their supply from slimy merchants.

Third, police and other law-enforcement authorities, domestic or   10
foreign, would be freed to deal with traditional nondrug crimes.

There are several objections that might be raised against such a   11
salutary solution.

First, it could be argued that by providing free drugs to the addict   12
we would consign him to permanent addiction. The answer is that medical and psychiatric help at the source would be more effective in controlling the addict's descent than the extremely limited remedies available to the victim today. I am not arguing that the new strategy will

cure everything. But I do not see many addicts being freed from their bonds under the present system.

In addition, as between the addict's predicament and the safety of 13 our innocent citizens, which deserves our primary concern? Drug-induced crime has become so common that almost every citizen knows someone in his immediate family or among his friends who has been mugged. It is these citizens who should be our chief concern.

Another possible objection is that addicts will cheat the system by 14 obtaining more than the allowable free shot. Without discounting the resourcefulness of the bedeviled addict, it should be possible to have Government cards issued that would be punched so as to limit the free supply in accord with medical authorization.

Yet all objections become trivial when matched against the crisis 15 itself. What we are witnessing is the demoralization of a great society: the ruination of its school children, athletes and executives, the corro-sion of the workforce in general.

Many thoughtful sociologists consider the rapidly spreading drug 16 use the greatest problem that our nation faces—greater and more real and urgent than nuclear bombs or economic reversal. In China, a simi-lar crisis drove the authorities to apply capital punishment to those who trafficked in opium—and extreme solution that arose from the deepest reaches of frustration.

Free drugs will win the war against the domestic terrorism caused 17 by illicit drugs. As a strategy, it is at once resourceful, sensible and simple. We are getting nowhere in our efforts to hold back the ocean of supply. The answer is to dry up demand.

Problems and Pain

M. SCOTT PECK

Life is difficult. 1

This is a great truth, one of the greatest truths. It is a great truth 2
because once we truly see this truth, we transcend it. Once we truly
know that life is difficult—once we truly understand and accept it—
then life is no longer difficult. Because once it is accepted, the fact that
life is difficult no longer matters.

Most do not fully see this truth that life is difficult. Instead they 3
moan more or less incessantly, noisily or subtly, about the enormity of
their problems, their burdens, and their difficulties as if life were generally easy, as if life *should* be easy. They voice their belief, noisily or
subtly, that their difficulties represent a unique kind of affliction that
should not be and that has somehow been especially visited upon them,
or else upon their families, their tribe, their class, their nation, their
race or even their species, and not upon others. I know about this
moaning because I have done my share.

Life is a series of problems. Do we want to moan about them or 4
solve them? Do we want to teach our children to solve them?

Discipline is the basic set of tools we require to solve life's problems. 5
Without discipline we can solve nothing. With only some discipline we
can solve only some problems. With total discipline we can solve all
problems.

What makes life difficult is that the process of confronting and 6
solving problems is a painful one. Problems, depending upon their nature, evoke in us frustration or grief or sadness or loneliness or guilt or
regret or anger or fear or anxiety or anguish or despair. These are
uncomfortable feelings, often very uncomfortable, often as painful as
any kind of physical pain, sometimes equaling the very worst kind of
physical pain. Indeed, it is *because* of the pain that events or conflicts
engender in us that we call them problems. And since life poses an
endless series of problems, life is always difficult and is full of pain as
well as joy.

Yet it is in this whole process of meeting and solving problems that 7
life has its meaning. Problems are the cutting edge that distinguishes

between success and failure. Problems call forth our courage and our wisdom; indeed, they create our courage and our wisdom. It is only because of problems that we grow mentally and spiritually. When we desire to encourage the growth of the human spirit, we challenge and encourage the human capacity to solve problems, just as in school we deliberately set problems for our children to solve. It is through the pain of confronting and resolving problems that we learn. As Benjamin Franklin said, "Those things that hurt, instruct." It is for this reason that wise people learn not to dread but actually to welcome problems and actually to welcome the pain of problems.

The Young and the Old

KONRAD LORENZ

*S*ince time immemorial, there have been conflicts between the young and   1
the old. How do you, Professor Lorenz, as an older person, as a scientist, and as
a human being, view this universal problem?

The young and the old have always been opposed. The old have   2
always advocated conservative principles while the young have always
lobbied for the new, for growth and development. Both are necessary
for the development of culture, just as genetic continuity and genetic
change are indispensable for the development of a species. Without
any change at all—without genetic change or without cultural revolutions—one is left with a living fossil, with a rigid system that cannot
develop.

However, when the conservative element is completely lacking, one   3
has "monsters" and "malformations." The continued existence—I don't
mean vegetative but the healthy, continued existence of a species or a
culture—is dependent on the existence of a healthy equilibrium between the elements of change that emanate from youth and the elements of conservatism that tend to be the province of older people. It is
certainly much harder to maintain this equilibrium today than it ever
was because our cultural development is accelerating exponentially,
which means that the cultural distance between the generations increases with each generation. The danger that development is too
rapid brings with it another very pernicious danger; namely that there
is a rupture in tradition. Many young people today are not aware of
how important tradition is or how much traditional knowledge is necessary for the healthy culture and social life of a nation or a people. On
the other hand, too many older people reject any change, which is
equally bad. What both the young and the old least like to hear is that
both are part of a so-called system of equipotential harmony that must
maintain an equilibrium so that the living system—and a culture is just
as much a living system as is an organism or a species—can continue to
exist.

Of course, youth has a harder time today. Older people under-   4

133

stand them less well; the enmity between the generations is very dangerous. This divergence is constantly increasing and can even lead to
the downfall of our culture. Young people must bear in mind that one
cannot simply "throw older people (instead of the baby) out with the
bath." We don't make it very easy for the young, and I understand that
the temptation to throw older people out is very great. Young people
notice very quickly that today's society is not always directed and gov-
erned by the people most worthy of our confidence, because, when you
come down to it, it isn't really the government that is at the helm.
Rather, it is the so-called lobbies—a synthesis of money men and political men. Such lobbyists are experts, professionals of their trade and are
utterly immoral.

If you take an individual executive of a multinational corporation, 5
you will most likely find him to be a solid, decent, kind man, one whom
I would immediately name the guardian of my children if I should die.
When sixty of these men gather in a board of directors meeting, however, they act as though they were intellectual criminals. Each one
alone is a charming old gentleman, utterly dependable, but together
they plan and build factories that are extremely dangerous and harmful for the environment. Not one of these gentleman has ever committed suicide, because the individual does not feel responsible for the
decisions of the group; and so it is around the world.

Now these lobbyists are, viewed collectively, not so stupid that they 6
can't foresee the dangers of their actions, nor are they so cruel that
they want to kill their own grandchildren by suffocation, poison, radio-
activity, or any of the other "nice things" that we have on earth. They
simply don't believe that the danger is *real*.

The Boy Who Drew Cats

LAFCADIO HEARN

A long, long time ago, in a small country village in Japan, there ₁ lived a poor farmer and his wife, who were very good people. They had a number of children, and found it very hard to feed them all. The elder son was strong enough when only fourteen years old to help his father; and the little girls learned to help their mother almost as soon as they could walk.

But the youngest, a little boy, did not seem to be fit for hard work. ₂ He was very clever—cleverer than all his brothers and sisters; but he was quite weak and small, and people said he could never grow very big. So his parents thought it would be better for him to become a priest than to become a farmer. They took him with them to the village-temple one day, and asked the good old priest who lived there if he would have their little boy for his acolyte, and teach him all that a priest ought to know.

The old man spoke kindly to the lad, and asked him some hard ₃ questions. So clever were the answers that the priest agreed to take the little fellow into the temple as an acolyte, and to educate him for the priesthood.

The boy learned quickly what the old priest taught him, and was ₄ very obedient in most things. But he had one fault. He liked to draw cats during study-hours, and to draw cats even where cats ought not to have been drawn at all.

Whenever he found himself alone, he drew cats. He drew them on ₅ the margins of the priest's books, and on all the screens of the temple, and on the walls, and on the pillars. Several times the priest told him this was not right; but he did not stop drawing cats. He drew them because he could not really help it. He had what is called "the genius of an artist," and just for that reason he was not quite fit to be an acolyte;—a good acolyte should study books.

One day after he had drawn some very clever pictures of cats upon ₆ a paper screen, the old priest said to him severely: "My boy, you must go away from this temple at once. You will never make a good priest, but perhaps you will become a great artist. Now let me give you a last

135

piece of advice, and be sure you never forget it. *Avoid large places at night;—keep to small!*"

They boy did not know what the priest meant by saying "*Avoid large places;—keep to small.*" He thought and thought, while he was tying up his little bundle of clothes to go away; but he could not understand those words, and he was afraid to speak to the priest any more, except to say goodby. 7

He left the temple very sorrowfully, and began to wonder what he should do. If he went straight home he felt sure his father would punish him for having been disobedient to the priest; so he was afraid to go home. All at once he remembered that at the next village, twelve miles away, there was a very big temple. He had heard there were several priests at that temple; and he made up his mind to go to them and ask them to take him for the acolyte. 8

Now that big temple was closed up but the boy did not know this fact. The reason it had been closed up was that a goblin had frightened the priests away, and had taken possession of the place. Some brave warriors had afterward gone to the temple at night to kill the goblin; but they had never been seen alive again. Nobody had ever told these things to the boy;—so he walked all the way to the village hoping to be kindly treated by the priests. 9

When he got to the village, it was already dark, and all the people were in bed; but he saw the big temple on a hill at the other end of the principal street, and he saw there was a light in the temple. People who tell the story say the goblin used to make that light, in order to tempt lonely travelers to ask for shelter. The boy went at once to the temple, and knocked. There was no sound inside. He knocked and knocked again; but still nobody came. At last he pushed gently at the door, and was quite glad to find that it had not been fastened. So he went in, and saw a lamp burning—but no priest. 10

He thought some priest would be sure to come very soon, and he sat down and waited. Then he noticed that everything in the temple was gray with dust, and thickly spun over with cobwebs. So he thought to himself that the priests would certainly like to have an acolyte, to keep the place clean. He wondered why they had allowed everything to get so dusty. What most pleased him, however, were some big white screens, good to paint cats upon. Though he was tired, he looked at once for a writing pad, and found one and ground some ink, and began to paint cats. 11

He painted a great many cats upon the screens; and then he began to feel very, very sleepy. He was just on the point of lying down to sleep beside one of the screens, when he suddenly remembered the words, "*Avoid large places;—keep to small!*" 12

The temple was very large; he was all alone; and as he thought of 13 these words—though he could not quite understand them—he began to feel for the first time a little afraid; and he resolved to look for a *small place* in which to sleep. He found a little cabinet, with a sliding door, and went into it, and shut himself up. Then he lay down and fell fast asleep.

Very late in the night he was awakened by a most terrible noise—a 14 noise of fighting and screaming. It was so dreadful that he was afraid even to look through a chink in the little cabinet; he lay very still, holding his breath for fright.

The light that had been in the temple went out; but the awful 15 sounds continued, and became more awful, and all the temple shook. After a long time silence came; but the boy was still afraid to move. He did not move until the light of the morning sun shone into the cabinet through the chinks of the little door.

Then he got out of his hiding place vary cautiously, and looked 16 about. The first thing he saw was that all the floor of the temple was covered with blood. And then he saw, lying dead in the middle of it, an enormous, monstrous rat—a goblin-rat—bigger than a cow!

But who or what could have killed it? There was no man or other 17 creature to be seen. Suddenly the boy observed that the mouths of all the cats he had drawn the night before, were red and wet with blood. Then he knew that the goblin had been killed by the cats which he had drawn. And then also, for the first time, he understood why the wise old priest had said to him; "*Avoid large places at night,—keep to small.*"

Afterward that boy became a very famous artist. Some of the cats 18 which he drew are still shown to travelers in Japan.

PART FOUR

Responding to Language

The readings in Part Four are about how language affects our attitudes and behavior. We are all "language experts" to some extent, because we spend so much of our time using language and responding to it. Based on your experiences, then, you probably will find yourself agreeing with some of the observations in these essays, disagreeing with some, and wondering about others. Whatever your responses, however, look on them as opportunities to explore how language affects your perceptions of yourself, other people, and the workings of society.

When we consider language as a broad subject, many possible writing topics arise. We may be moved to write directly about the effects that certain kinds of words or phrases have on us. At other times, we may want to delve into how language affects our cultural and social experiences, such as the effects of advertising language or bureaucratic jargon. And there is always the strong possibility that reading about language may generate responses that have little to do with the direct concerns of a particular author. Your immediate responses to these readings should indicate what kinds of feelings are aroused when you read about language, and this should lead you to express yourself in language of your own.

Small-fry Swearing

SUSAN FERRARO

I got back from Saturday morning errands to find the kitchen humming with excitement. "Our son got asked out by a girl," my husband said, for once coming straight to the point.

I'd heard about girls calling boys, and I wasn't worried: Matt is 11 years old. "Are you going?" I asked him, brimming with supercool momism.

"No," he said. "I told her I was busy this weekend."

"It's better not to hurt her feelings," I began to say.

"So this other girl gets on the phone," he rushed on, "and she says, if I won't go out with the first one, will I take her to the movies instead?"

"What?"

"And I said, well, no, I didn't go out yet, so they asked if I was gay."

"What?"

"I said no, I'm not gay, I just don't go out, so they told me to go . . . and hung up."

"What?"

There was a lot wrong with this, but what struck me was the language. Adults have a hard time believing it, but children today—from nice families and good schools—often use coarse, ugly language, full of sexual insults. They get it from movies, cable television, rap, friends, and mostly from the street. Boys, it seems, have always had access to this vocabulary; what comes as a surprise is that these days girls use "bad" language too.

As far as I know, my kids don't swear. But given the world we live in (a nice-enough New York suburb), if they want to tell me what really started the fight that has triggered a trip to the nurse and a call from the vice principal, they need to convey the full flavor and specificity of playground exchange. We use simple codes for unprintable words—precious, I admit, but preferable to having the house resound with street language.

In the kitchen, our thirteen-year-old daughter took up the narrative: "They called nine times. When I answered they told me to tell my brother what to do with himself again, and hung up." A sister's smile flitted across her face.

"I asked them," Matt said, "'How many of you girls are there   14 pestering me?' and they laughed and said 10. It was a sleep-over."

Matt had told his story well, but he looked a little pale. After we   15 concocted some verbal slam-dunks for future use ("Hey, do you *eat* with that mouth?"), he took a deep breath: "Is there something wrong with me that I don't want to go out yet?" Of course we said no—he was normal! They were obnoxious!—but he looked unconvinced as he slouched off to play with G.I. Joes.

The small-fry swearing I'd heard previously had been confined to   16 all-girl or all-boy groups. Were the she-puppies from hell who were yapping at my son's heels typical, or was he the target of an unusually nasty group? Where were their mothers while this was going on? Visions of my son made combative and hostile by vile encounters with girls—girls who seemed to fulfill a misogynist's nightmare of the sexually aggressive, emasculating female—swam before my eyes.

I called a friend, Allen Gold, a school psychologist from Marin   17 County, Calif., who has made preadolescent psyches his lifework. Yes, he said with a sigh, girls do sometimes talk like that to boys: "They want to talk like adults, but they don't know how." Boys are not much more contained about verbal abuse, he added; they often use vulgar language ("slut" is especially popular right now) to describe girls who are not present to other girls. "But boys are more spontaneous," he said. "If something bugs them, they might call a girl something to her face."

While some mothers may remain blissfully ignorant of what is   18 going on, many are aware. "I know my daughter and her friends talk like that on the telephone," the mother of an 11-year-old girl told me. "But I feel it's an invasion of her privacy to monitor or intervene in her phone calls."

In the milder age I grew up in, we called this baloney. Nine years   19 ago, this woman taught her daughter not to hit other children; why abdicate responsibility now? One friend says it is because mothers are afraid their daughters won't like them otherwise. That may be true (in which case, they are abdicating parenthood altogether), but as the mother of a daughter as well as a son, I wonder.

When my generation arrived on the adult scene 20 years ago, we   20 were sick of sexually stereotyped, suffocating double standards. Could men do their own laundry? Yes. Could women compete? Yes. Could women use what was until then all-male (and, not coincidentally, all-powerful) vocabulary—i.e., swear? Yes. For women, "nice" language was like sitting at home waiting for the phone to ring—it symbolized what had held us back and what we had been denied, what made us second-class citizens.

Now we are the standard-bearers for our daughters. I swear, and 21
my children hear me. When I tell them not to, especially when I tell my daughter not to, hypocrisy tugs at my sleeve. Am I sticking her in the same mess of double standards from which I tried so hard to escape? It feels culturally wrong to me as a woman and personally dishonest to impose rules on her that I felt such justification and joy in dismissing.

Sixth-grade girls have always been, for boys, hard to take: as a 22
group, they are two years ahead in sexual development (a fact that is all too visible in their figures) and six inches taller. Longing for the dance floor, but with one foot still in the sandbox, they are as likely to slug a classmate as smile at him. If girls talk like tough, sexually demanding women—"are you gay?"—won't boys fall back on defensive contempt, and prefer male-only company? Won't they counterattack with anti-female language (which, if memory serves, tends to surpass in crudity and variety what women say, even today)?

Won't they do exactly what we've been trying to get them not to do 23
for the last 20 years?

We walk a fine line between then and now when we teach our 24
daughters to be nice, to be good. It is half a step from nice to passive. Growing up, many of us heard "Be a good girl!" so often that it was with us for years, an ancient chorus of elders that replayed, like irritating elevator music, long after we'd got out on the floor of adulthood.

But to the mothers of daughters as well as sons I sound an alarm. 25
Words matter, restraint is not always confinement, and one double standard that makes sense is that what works for adults does not always work for children. It is possible to tell them, girls and boys: I can say things as an adult that you, because you are a child, cannot.

At our house, Matt has built a wall of defense against almost every- 26
thing female. "Not all girls are like that," I told him one afternoon. "Someday you're going to meet great girls, ones you like." He eyed me skeptically. "Look," I said. "I was a little girl once, right? And I'm O.K., right?"

"Nice try, mom." His words and tone were the same that I use 27
when he has tried to float an especially absurd excuse past me. "They are trying to make up my life for me," he said, referring to what sounded like almost daily attempts to draw him into the social whirl. "They want to know if I like one of them in particular."

"And?"   28

"I told them I didn't because she used curse words when my sister 29
answered the phone that time."

"And?"   30

"I went out to shoot baskets with the guys."   31

SAMPLE RESPONSES to "Small-fry Swearing"

Responder 1: George —————————————————

This woman wants us to believe she is concerned only about other children's welfare, but I think she is just out of step with modern ways of talking. I bet her son feels she is being too uptight, and he probably resents her trying to be his buddy by defending him against those "she–puppies from hell." Heck, my grandmother would not let anyone say "hell," much less write the word, or any other curse word. She believed that cursing shows disrespect for God and reveals a sinful, or at least lazy, brain. I'm sure this writer would argue that Granma was <u>too</u> uptight and that she should relax and accept the idea that women have a right to express themselves forcefully, especially when trying to hold their own in a man's world. Actually, we are talking about a thin gray line between what is "not quite nice" and what is "going too far." The line has moved quite a bit since Granma was a girl, but that does not mean the world is going to the Devil.

Responder 2: Elizabeth —————————————————

I think this woman is right. I feel very uncomfortable when I am in the movies with a boy or even with my girl friends. The language is awful. In old

movies they used to find words that let us know how angry
or tough the characters were without filling their
mouths with filthy obscenities. I wish we still had
censors to force the movies to clean up their act. The
rating system doesn't help at all.

Of course, movies also show men and women doing gross
things to each other, acting as if everyone who is with
it would want to make love as though they were starring
in a movie. I guess they make movies this way to make
money from teenage boys who want to feel they are grown
up or want to learn how to turn girls on. The trouble is
they think that what they see in the movies is real cool,
and when they go out on dates, they talk dirty and expect
the girls to jump in bed with them and act dirty. And the
girls who watch these movies come to think they have to
do the same thing if they want to get boys to like them.
As this writer points out, all this sick behavior starts
very early these days.

Responder 3: Bobby —————————————————

What does it matter what words you use? When you're
angry, you curse. Men use rougher language, but when
someone is angry at you and curses you out, you feel it
just as bad no matter what particular words they use.
Those little girls wanted to break her son's chops, so
they used the most painful words they knew. They
probably heard them in the movies or on TV, or maybe they
got them from an older brother or even their parents. So
what? This lady probably did the same thing when she was

young; only she called the boy a "sissy" or "mama's boy"
instead of "faggot." But to the kids, it's the same
idea.

My girl has a real bad mouth. Man she really lets me
have it sometimes. But I know she's just pissed off at me
and we'll be back in love again as soon as it all blows
over. She's better off letting her feelings out than if
she kept all that garbage inside. I don't let her words
bother me. Besides I let her hear a few choice words when
I get mad about something.

CONSIDERING THE RESPONSES

Responder 1: George

Most of the class thought George had found an easy topic: showing how the passage of time brings changes in what is generally considered normal or acceptable behavior, especially in the area of language. However, is the "easy topic" really all that easy to develop into an essay? How heavily could George rely on examples of shifts in what was considered "bad language" in Granma's day and what is unacceptable in the 1990s? Could readers reasonably expect George to offer his opinion as to why these changes are taking place so rapidly? Would you advise George to shift his focus to the question of whether the most recent changes are harmful to society? (He said we are not going to Hell yet.) What do you think of one student's suggestion that George examine the writer's relationship with her son?

Responder 2: Elizabeth

Elizabeth's response drew a variety of comments from her classmates, who saw a number of topics she could profitably pursue. One idea which received a great deal of support from her peers was to explore the effect of the movies in shaping young people's attitudes toward love and sexuality. Think of a thesis for such an essay, and briefly sketch out a line of reasoning that would develop that thesis.

Responder 3: Bobby ───────────────────────────────────

The class quickly noted that Bobby had uncovered two distinctly different topics: the actual effect that words have on most people, and, the benefits of employing violent language to express feelings and thereby to create an honest, healthy relationship. The interest of the class pointed toward the question whether or not violent language serves as a beneficial cathartic, flushing out the poisonous feelings of the moment so that a relationship can stay healthy. What is your opinion on this question? Can either position be defended effectively except by citing one's own relationships, as Bobby did in his response?

Words as Weapons

RICHARD MITCHELL

Imagine that the postman brings you a letter from the Water and 1
Sewer Department or the Bureau of Mines or some such place. Any
right-thinking American will eye even the envelope in the same way he
would eye some sticky substance dripping from the underparts of his
automobile. Things get worse. You open the letter and see at once these
words: "You are hereby notified. . . ." How do you feel? Are you keen
to read on? But you will, won't you? Oh, yes. You will.

Here comes another letter. This one doesn't even have a stamp. It 2
carries instead the hint that something very bad will happen to any
mere citizen caught using this envelope for his own subversive purposes. You open it and read: "It has been brought to the attention of
this office. . . ." Do you throw it out at that point because you find it too
preposterous to think that an office can have an attention? Do you
immediately write a reply: "Dear So-and-so, I am surprised and dis-
tressed by the rudeness of your first ten words, especially since they are
addressed to one of those who pay your salary. Perhaps you're having a
bad day. Why don't you write again and say something else?" You do
not. In fact, you turn pale and wonder frantically which of your mis-
deeds has been revealed. Your anxiety is increased by that passive
verb—that's what it's for—which suggests that this damaging exposure
has been made not by an envious neighbor or a vengeful merchant or
an ex-girlfriend or any other perfectly understandable, if detestable,
human agent, but by the very nature of the universe. "It has been
brought." This is serious.

Among the better class of Grammarians, that construction is known 3
as the Divine Passive. It intends to suggest that neither the writer nor
anyone else through whose head you might like to hammer a blunt
wooden spike can be held accountable for anything in any way. Like an
earthquake or a volcanic eruption, this latest calamity must be accepted
as an act of God. God may well be keeping count of the appearances of
the Divine Passive.

Another classic intimidation with which to begin a letter is: "Ac- 4
cording to our records. . . ." It reminds you at once, with that plural

147

pronoun, that the enemy outnumbers you, and the reference to "records" makes it clear that they've got the goods. There is even a lofty pretense to fairness, as though you were being invited to bring forth *your* records to clear up this misunderstanding. You know, however, that they don't suspect for an instant that there's anything wrong in their records. Besides, you don't *have* any records, as they damn well know.

Such frightening phrases share an important attribute. They are 5 not things that ordinary people are likely to say, or even write, to one another except, of course, in certain unpleasant circumstances. We can see their intentions when we put them into more human contexts: "My dear Belinda, You are hereby notified . . ." conveys a message that ought to infuriate even the dullest of Belindas. Why is it then that we are not infuriated when we hear or read such words addressed to us by bureaucrats? We don't even stop to think that those words make up a silly verbal paradox; the only context in which they can possibly appear is the one in which they are not needed at all. No meaning is added to "Your rent is overdue" when the landlord writes, "You are hereby notified that your rent is overdue." What *is* added is the tone of official legality, and the presumption that one of the rulers is addressing one of the ruled. The voice . . . puts you in your place, and, strangely enough, you go there.

We Americans make much of our egalitarian society, and we like to 6 think we are not intimidated by wealth and power. Still, we are. There are surely many reasons for that, and about most of them we can do nothing, it seems. But one of the reasons is the very language in which the wealthy and powerful speak to us. When we hear it, something ancient stirs in us, and we take off our caps and hold them to our chests as we listen. About *that* we *could* do something—all it takes is some education. That must have been in Jefferson's mind when he thought about the importance of universal education in a society of free people. People who are automatically and unconsciously intimidated by the sound of a language that they cannot themselves use easily will never be free. Jefferson must have imagined an America in which all citizens would be able, when they felt like it, to address one another as members of the same class. That we cannot do so is a sore impediment to equality, but, of course, a great advantage to those who *can* use the English of power and wealth.

It would be easier to see bureaucratic language for what it is if only 7 the governors and bureaucrats did in fact speak a foreign tongue. When the Normans ruled England anyone could tell the French was French and English, English. It was the government that might, rarely, pardon you for your crimes, but it needed a friend to forgive you for your sins. Words like "pardon" and "forgive" were clearly in different languages, and, while either might have been translated by the other, they still meant subtly different acts. They still do, even though they are both thought of as English words now. Modern English has swallowed up many such distinctions, but not all. We still know that hearts are broken, not fractured. This is the kind of distinction Winston Churchill had in mind when he advised writers to choose the native English word whenever possible rather than a foreign import. This is good advice, but few can heed it in these days. The standard American education does not provide the knowledge out of which to make such choices.

SAMPLE RESPONSES to "Words as Weapons"

Responder 1: Marlene

I know how this writer feels. I got a letter from a department store that said I owed them fifteen dollars. The way they wrote the letter, you would have thought I owed them a million dollars. They used legal words, just like the ones the writer talks about——"You are hereby informed." The letter made me mad because I've bought a lot of things on credit at that store, and I've always paid my bills. I didn't even know I owed the money. You'd think that with my good record they could have sent a nicer letter. Instead they made me feel like some kind of crook. I should have sent them back a nasty letter, but I didn't. I just paid what I owed. I should have read this essay before. Then I might have sent them a nasty letter. This essay really taught me something.

Responder 2: Harry

I say baloney to this essay. I owned a store for
fifteen years in my old neighborhood. When I started
out, I was Mr. Nice Guy. People would come into my store
and ask for credit. They looked honest and nice, and
they gave me some story about not having had a chance to
get to the bank. They were always going to pay me
tomorrow or in a couple of days. I played the sucker for
so long that I was going into debt myself. When I finally
wised up, I changed my attitude. I got tough with the
deadbeats and told them, "No cash, no merchandise."
People who owed me a lot, I threatened to get the law
after them. You'd be surprised how fast all the
parasites found out that they had money after all.
That's why companies send letters like the ones the
author says are so insulting to people. That's just too
bad! If you don't scare the hell out of people, they'll
never pay what they owe. I'm sixty-six years old, and
one thing I've learned is that when it comes to money,
you've got to be tough. Otherwise you'll go down the
drain.

Responder 3: Leon

What's all this talk about English and writing?
That's all I've heard since I started school. Teachers
always talk about how important good English is, but who
cares! I want to be an accountant. I do very good in

accounting classes. I wish they'd stop wasting my time with all this required English. All I want to do is graduate and get a good job. I don't know what this guy is talking about with his "Divine Passive" and all that crap. If they forgot about all this English, I could graduate and get out of here a lot faster, and start making some money. So I'll never know how to write like a great writer--so what! As long as I do my job OK and make good money, everybody's happy. That's all I've got to say.

Responder 4: Caron

I see the author's point, and he's probably right when he says the wealthy and powerful use a certain kind of language to keep the rest of us in line. In fact language is used to separate classes and professions too. Middle-class people speak differently than lower-class people. Doctors and lawyers have their own languages. They use words that most people don't understand, and in this way they make it impossible for us to do without them. But I don't know if it would make a difference if all of us used ordinary language. A rich and powerful man would still be respected and feared even if he spoke like an ordinary person. Sometimes politicians try to get people to vote for them by talking like Mr. or Mrs. Average Citizen. To me, they always sound phony. I can tell they're putting on an act to win votes.

CONSIDERING THE RESPONSES

Response 1: Marlene

Marlene ended her response by saying: "This essay really taught me something." Based on Marlene's complete response, what do you think she meant by her last statement? Could the statement be used as the controlling idea for a complete essay? Why or why not? If Marlene decides to write about what she learned from this essay, how could she use the essay itself to help plan her own essay?

Response 2: Harry

Harry's response was based on his experience as a store owner. Evidently this helped to shape his attitudes about creditors and made him sympathetic toward the kind of threatening language the author wants us to resist. During class discussion Harry said several times: "Business is business." How might Harry develop an essay explaining what he means by "Business is business"? What kinds of explanatory support might he include besides his experiences as a store owner? How would you argue *against* the idea that humane considerations should have no place in business?

Response 3: Leon

Leon apparently thinks that required English courses have little value for him, since he wants to pursue a career in accounting. His response led the class to discuss the value of courses that are not directly related to a student's major field of study. Students argued that employers favor people who write and speak well and, furthermore, that getting ahead in a career often has as much to do with communication skills as with knowledge of the particular field. Leon claimed that he had no ambitions to be a boss or an executive, and he doubted that he would ever use language well enough to be considered "executive material." All he wanted, he maintained, was the chance to get a decent job so that he could get married, buy a house, and drive a sports car. Leon decided to write an essay supporting his views about "useless" courses. Do you think he explored enough issues in his response and in class discussion to develop an effective essay? Why or why not? Which of Leon's arguments is strongest, and why? Which is weakest, and why?

Response 4: Caron

Caron raised two issues. First she wrote about how language is used to separate people into different classes and different professions. Then she questioned the idea that the use of ordinary language by everyone would create a more democratic society. Which of these two issues would be easier to explore in an essay? Why? Depending on your this question how should Caron develop her essay?

Children's Insults

PETER FARB

The insults spoken by adults are usually more subtle than the simple name-calling used by children, but children's insults make obvious some of the verbal strategies people carry into adult life. Most parents engage in wishful thinking when they regard name-calling as good-natured fun which their children will soon grow out of. Name-calling is not good-natured and children do not grow out of it; as adults they merely become more expert in its use. Nor is it true that "sticks and stones may break my bones, but names will never hurt me." Names can hurt very much because children seek out the victim's true weakness, then jab exactly where the skin is thinnest. Name-calling can have major impact on a child's feelings about his identity, and it can sometimes be devastating to his psychological development.

Almost all examples of name-calling by children fall into four categories:

1. Names based on physical peculiarities, such as deformities, use of eyeglasses, racial characteristics, and so forth. A child may be called *Flattop* because he was born with a misshapen skull—or, for obvious reasons, *Fat Lips, Gimpy, Four Eyes, Peanuts, Fatso, Kinky*, and so on.
2. Names based on a pun or parody of the child's own name. Children with last names like Fitts, McClure, and Farb usually find them converted to *Shits, Manure*, and *Fart*.
3. Names based on social relationships. Examples are *Baby* used by a sibling rival or *Chicken Shit* for someone whose courage is questioned by his social group.
4. Names based on mental traits—such as *Clunkhead, Dummy, Jerk*, and *Smartass*.

These four categories were listed in order of decreasing offensiveness to the victims. Children regard names based on physical peculiarities as the most cutting, whereas names based on mental traits are, surprisingly, not usually regarded as very offensive. Most children are very vulnerable to names that play upon the child's rightful name—no doubt because one's name is a precious possession, the mark of a unique identity and one's masculinity or femininity. Those American Indian tribes that had the custom of never revealing true names undoubtedly avoided considerable psychological damage.

SAMPLE RESPONSES to "Children's Insults"

Responder 1: Larry

I remember a fat boy named Ralph who used to live in our neighborhood. My friends and I always referred to him as Fatty or The Whale. I don't know why he hung out with us, except maybe he was lonely and hoped we would eventually accept him. We were pretty nasty kids. We never stopped teasing Ralph, and I have to admit we really enjoyed it. We would make up jokes about how fat he was, and we played a lot of dirty tricks on him. When he finally blew up or started crying, we'd get even meaner, calling him much worse names.

I guess our insults really got to him because one day he ran away from home. It took the police a couple of days to find him. To tell the truth, we didn't feel bad about what happened to Ralph. In fact, we thought the whole thing was a terrific joke. I went around saying the police would have no trouble finding Ralph since he was too fat to hide for very long.

When I think about it now, I feel bad about how cruel we were to Ralph. But I sure didn't feel sorry for him at

the time. I guess the writer is right when he says little
children can be vicious.

Responder 2: Alice

I try to teach my daughter that it is a sin to say
anything derogatory about another human being. The Lord
does not want us to insult each other. But she tells me
all the other children in her school use insults all the
time, and she will occasionally hurt another child's
feelings right before my eyes. Sometimes I think it is a
hopeless task to be a parent these days. Between the
influence of television and other children, I feel that
I don't have much to say about the way my daughter is
growing up. She already uses language that makes me
blush. What will she be saying in another five years,
when she is a teenager?

Responder 3: Donald

This writer referred to the old saying about sticks
and stones; however, I believe he is not entirely
correct. The surest remedy for an insult is to totally
ignore it. When somebody attempts to unnerve me by using
words like "stupid" or "asshole," I content myself with
the thought that the words better describe the speaker.
Ignoring such people works surprisingly well. If you
remain unflustered, they will soon move on to another,
more easily upset victim.

CONSIDERING THE RESPONSES

Response 1: Larry

Larry's response struck a familiar chord in the class. Nearly everyone recalled being either the insulter or the insulted in grade school, and in most cases the insults were aimed at some physical trait. Given Larry's generalization that children can be vicious, do you think that his essay should focus only on Ralph or on a number of examples to prove the point? Why? If Larry includes examples other than Ralph in his essay, should he explore *why* he and his friends were so mean, or will the examples alone prove that children are "vicious"?

Response 2: Alice

Alice's response offers several fertile topics for an essay, but the class immediately focused on her fear that as a parent she had too little control over her daughter's moral development. What does Alice need to do if she decides to write about the "hopeless task" of being a parent? What advice would you give her?

Response 3: Donald

No one in the class seemed to agree with Donald's method of handling verbal assaults. They said it would never work to ignore insults. Donald viewed their reactions as a challenge that he gladly accepted. What should Donald do to expand his response into an effective essay? Will the use of examples prove his point? Why or why not? Do you see any way that Donald can support his claim that "the surest remedy for an insult is to totally ignore it"?

Parallel Speaking and Real Conversation

THEODORE ISAAC RUBIN

There is a kind of conversation that I call *parallel speaking,* 1
which leads to a sense of nonconnection, frustration, and "having nothing to say to each other." This is of course a spoiler of love.

In parallel speaking, each person goes on saying what he or she has 2
to say by turn *without bouncing off each other*. It is as if he or she has his
or her speech to make and waits politely or otherwise for the other to
finish so that he can add to his own speech. This is not dialogue. No
matter how much information is given and how well each person listens, this is not fruitful, love-enhancing conversation.

In real conversation, cross-associations constantly take place. This 3
means that each time one person says something, the other person is
stimulated by what is said, has associations to what is said, states them,
and the first person does the same thing.

In other words, loving, involved people respond to each other's 4
talk producing a common set of ideas to which each has contributed in
response to each other.

This talk is an extension of feelings. These feelings and their ex- 5
pressions are inspired by each other in a real conversation—the antith-
esis of parallel speaking, which is isolated talk even though two people
may be together and even listening.

SAMPLE RESPONSES to "Parallel Speaking and Real Conversation"

Responder: Janine _____

This writer seems to be describing the way my
parents talk with me and my brother. Occasionally we try

to let them know how we feel about events going on in our lives, but they don't let us get to the point. They step right into the conversation and tell us what they think we should be thinking. Dad will deliver a speech about "young people today," and Mother recalls how in high school she and her friends handled whatever problem I was trying to discuss. It is usually hard to get back into a conversation once they have interrupted, but when I finally do, they just sit there politely waiting for me to hesitate slightly so they can return to their monologues.

I used to think this was a sign of the generation gap, but that is not the case. My friend Ann's mother always makes us feel that she is truly interested in our opinions and that she values our sharing our feelings and observations with her. Ann says her mother is her closest friend. I realize that my mother loves me, but I'd never say she is my best friend. She and Dad are just too caught up in themselves to listen well to me.

Responder 2: Kristy

I think all adults do this. All they want to do is control our lives. They don't understand us. They think everything we do is wrong. My Mom does nothing but lecture me about the way I dress and boys and not getting pregnant. She never listens to me when I try to explain things to her. I think parents are like this because of the generation gap. They don't approve of our music or our clothes or our friends or anything else we do. They

forget that their parents didn't understand them, and
they don't even try to understand us. Every time I talk
to them I feel totally frustrated. I guess it's just
that the older generation doesn't have anything in
common with us.

Responder 3: Peter ────────────────────────────

This concept can be applied to teachers: good ones
listen to their students' ideas and allow discussions to
follow students' interests. Poor teachers give the
impression that their own ideas are far superior to
those of mere students; so, they keep on lecturing even
during what are supposed to be discussion periods. It is
sad to say, but most of the teachers I have known do not
seem very interested in their students except as
audiences for their opinions.

The most frustrating teachers are those who seem to
want to dialogue with students, but they cannot relate
to student interests. When we want to discuss some
problem on campus, they take the topic back to the
national scene where their interests and expertise lie.
When we give our views on that national situation, they
interrupt, sometimes rather politely, to enlighten us
with their expert opinion, completely ignoring the
points we had raised. I learn the most from teachers who
pick up on my ideas and encourage me to develop my ideas
in light of their reactions to me.

CONSIDERING THE RESPONSES

Responder 1: Janine ————————————————

The whole class echoed Janine's view of adults as conversational partners, saying that very few seemed genuinely interested in their children's ideas. How could Janine go about defending her position, that the problem in communication grows out of individual self-centeredness rather than the simple passing of the years? Would she have to rely entirely upon the example of her friend's mother? Would her paper be effective if she merely collected other examples?

Responder 2: Kristy ————————————————

Did Kristy stick to the topic of parallel conversations between two people trying to relate lovingly with each other? Is conversation the true focus of her interest in this response? Do you feel Kristy was right about her having nothing in common with persons her parents' age? In what ways could Kristy define the conflict between herself and her parents more clearly?

Responder 3: Peter ————————————————

Peter has taken the topic into another area of interest. Is there a significant connection between "loving, involved people" and the teacher-student relationship? How can Peter avoid being too general in his treatment of his topic? Would examples be very helpful here? Should Peter delve into the reasons why teachers might tend to be wary of following students' leads in classroom discussions?

ADDITIONAL READINGS

Talking Like a Lady: How Women Talk

FRANCINE FRANK
FRANK ANSHEN

Perhaps the most common stereotype about women's speech is 1
that women talk a lot. If we take "a lot" to mean more than men, we are
faced with the surprising fact that there seems to be no study which
supports this belief, while there are several which show just the opposite. One such study, by Otto Sonder, Jr., is particularly interesting.
Sonder organized discussion groups which included women and men
and assigned them specific topics. The discussions were recorded and
transcribed, but in the transcripts, the participants were identified only
by letters, as A, B, etc. Panels of judges who tried to identify the sex of
each speaker from these transcripts were correct about fifty-five percent of the time, a result which is better than chance, but not overwhelmingly so. Closer examination of the data, however, reveals some
interesting facts. A word count of the recorded discussions showed a
clear tendency for the men who participated in the study to utter more
words than the women. In other words, men, on the average, actually
talked more than did women. Even more interesting is the fact that
individuals of either sex who talked a lot were more likely to be judged
as males, while taciturn individuals of either sex were more likely to be
identified as females. Not only does this study suggest that men are
more talkative, it also suggests that the judges "knew" this fact and used
it to make judgments about the sexual identity of unknown speakers.

162

Although, consciously, they would probably subscribe to the cultural stereotype of the talkative woman, their judgments show that they knew that the real situation is the direct opposite of the stereotype.

How can we reconcile this apparent contradiction between our beliefs and our actions? It seems that people have an incorrect conscious stereotype of how much women and men talk, while at the same time having, at a less conscious level, the knowledge that men tend to speak more than women. When called upon to make judgments, they use their knowledge of actual behavior rather than the stereotype of presumed behavior. We are reminded of individuals in pre-Civil War America who thought slaves were lazy, in spite of the fact that they observed them doing backbreaking work from sunup to sundown. 2

Students of stereotypes believe that our preconceived notions influence our expectations and responses during initial contacts with strangers. However, when we get to know people even slightly, we usually treat them as individuals and ignore the stereotypes. This is commonly recognized as the "Some of my best friends are . . ." syndrome. We may, for example, believe that girls are, in general, more social than boys, even though that may not be true of our own children or, indeed, of any children we know well; or we may believe that women are more talkative than men, although members of our family or circle of friends do not act that way. 3

How Fathers Talk to Babies

BARRY McLAUGHLIN

Much of what we know about the way children learn language   1
comes from studies in which researchers observe mothers with their
babies. . . . When mothers speak to their young children, their speech
becomes slower, shorter, less complex, more repetitious, uses fewer
pronouns. In fact, this way of talking is often called motherese.

Little is known about how fathers talk to babies, but one study indi-   2
cates they do not say much. Every two weeks during the first three
months of 10 babies' lives, Freda Rebelsky and Cheryl Hanks recorded
everything fathers said to their infants in a 24-hour period. The fathers spoke to them an average of merely 38 seconds.

One of the few studies concerned with fathers' speech to young   3
children was conducted by William Corsaro of Indiana University, who
found that fathers asked more questions than did mothers during interactions with their two-year-olds. Nearly half of the fathers' utterances were leading questions: What is this? (no response). Is this a
camel? (no response). Can you say that, camel? (no response). Camel?

Placed in the same situation, the children's mothers devoted only   4
18 percent of their utterances to questions of this sort. Such questions
are one of the safest routes adults can take in conversation with small
children. By asking leading questions, the adult feels comfortable with
the child and controls the conversation.

The father's tendency to use a controlling language style with   5
young children has been borne out of recent research I conducted with
Caleb Schutz and David White. We found that fathers used significantly more imperatives with their five-year-old children than mothers
did in the same situation.

In our experiment we recorded the conversations of 24 parents   6
and their children while they were playing a table game called Capture
the Hat. The game was new to the children, and the parents had to
teach them the rules. What struck us immediately was the difference in
teaching styles between the mothers and fathers. Mothers were involved with the children, they were careful about making rules clear,
and they corrected mistakes and rule infractions. Fathers, on the other

164

hand, were less involved; they often failed to cover the rules and tended to gloss over the children's mistakes or infractions. Although there were exceptions. Fathers seemed uncomfortable and intent on getting the game over with. In fact, we found it difficult to find fathers who would participate in the study.

When playing the game, fathers appeared uncertain as to how to 7 talk to their children. They often talked down to them, saying "All right, say you roll five. How would you move? Show me how many you would move. You would like this: One, two, three, four, five." In contrast, mothers tended to say the same thing more succinctly and less condescendingly: "Now, whatever number comes on the die, you get to move one of your hats that many places." Mothers did not count aloud because they knew the children could count spaces on a game board.

Although some fathers used speech that was too simple, under- 8 estimating what their children understood, others used language that was too advanced. In such cases the children did not understand the game, but their fathers' concern was not to explain it; they wanted to get it over with. These fathers glanced around uncomfortably, allowed rules to be broken, and seemed generally uninterested in the task.

Indirect information on the way fathers talk to young children 9 comes from a study by Elaine Andersen at Stanford University who had children aged between three and six play the role of parents. When the children pretended to be the father, their speech became shorter, their intonation changed (it became deeper, with less range in pitch), and they used more imperatives and fewer terms of endearment than when they played the mother.

> **Experimenter** (taking the child's role): Tell me a story.
>
> **Child** (in father's role): Mommy will.
>
> **Experimenter:** No, I want you to.
>
> **Child:** I'm going to sleep.
>
> **Experimenter:** Please tell me a story.
>
> **Child:** Ask your mother.
>
> **Experimenter:** Please, please.
>
> **Child:** All right. Sit down. Once upon a time. The end.

Other research suggests that the language of fathers to their children is less attuned to the child's needs than is the speech of mothers. Fathers neither repeat nor expand the speech of young children who are learning to talk to the same extent that mothers do. Fathers are generally less skilled in motherese, although there has been so little research on fathers' speech to young children that we do not know, for example, whether this is true of fathers who are equally involved with the mothers in the child's upbringing. It appears that as long as most fathers leave the business of bringing up children to the mother, the language to which infants are exposed will continue to be principally the "mother tongue."

Saying It May Make It So

JOHN C. CONDON, JR.

It is clear that a person's attitude, self-esteem, and behavior can 1
be affected by the label the person has come to accept. It is also possible
that large numbers of other people, entire institutions, even events in
history can be altered in part by what is said about them.

In 1982, a syndicated stock market analyst predicted that the stock 2
market would drop significantly, and so recommended to his large
number of readers that they sell quickly. Two things happened. His
readers and many others who heard his prediction did sell; and, as
predicted, the prices of stocks plunged. One interpretation is that the
adviser had the foresight to see what was going to happen, and he had
the facilities to warn his followers. Another interpretation is that because so many people thought the market would drop, they quickly
sold, which itself caused the market to drop. This latter interpretation
is an example of what has come to be known as the "self-fulfilling
prophecy," a phenomenon first identified by sociologist Robert K. Mer-
ton.

Note that the self-fulfilling prophecy works only when the area 3
about which the prediction is made may, in some way, be acted upon by
the person making the prediction. It does not apply to statements like
"It will not rain tomorrow."

The potential of the self-fulfilling prophecy is extraordinary. Sup- 4
pose, for example, you label students on your campus or neighbors in
an apartment building you have just moved into *unfriendly*. Your label
is itself a kind of prediction: it suggests what kind of behavior you may
and may not expect from the others. How, then, should you act, if what
you predict is accurate? You certainly should not bother going out of
your way to be friendly yourself. And if others perceive your behavior
accordingly you will find that sure enough, the people just aren't
friendly.

In some stunning research conducted in the 1970s, it was found 5
that teachers can easily get the kind of performance from students that
they expect. Students were randomly divided into groups which were
then arbitrarily identified as either exceptionally good students or as

167

mediocre or poor students. In fact, there was no demonstrable difference, and of course nothing was said about this to the students themselves. The research showed clearly that when teachers thought their students were bright and eager, the students tended to act that way. When teachers were led to believe that their students were of lesser ability, the students tended to perform that way. The reasons lay not in the students, but rather in the students' responses to the teachers who unwittingly communicated different expectations based on what they had been told.

Reasons for a person's failing at any number of things—failing an   6
examination, losing a game, giving up trying to do something—are likely to include some influence of the self-fulfilling prophecy. If you have a test in the morning and you predict you cannot pass, then it is only smart not to bother studying. And not studying is very likely to help your prediction to come true. If a team knows it can't win, it is less likely to try and thus very likely to cause the prediction to come true.

The Test

ANGELICA GIBBS

On the afternoon Marian took her second driver's test, Mrs. 1
Ericson went with her. "It's probably better to have someone a little
older with you," Mrs. Ericson said as Marian slipped into the driver's
seat beside her. "Perhaps the last time your Cousin Bill made you nervous, talking too much on the way."

"Yes, Ma'am," Marian said in her soft unaccented voice. "They 2
probably do like it better if a white person shows up with you."

"Oh, I don't think it's *that*," Mrs. Ericson began, and subsided after 3
a glance at the girl's set profile. Marian drove the car slowly through
the shady suburban streets. It was one of the first hot days in June, and
when they reached the boulevard they found it crowded with cars
headed for the beaches.

"Do you want me to drive?" Mrs. Ericson asked. "I'll be glad to if 4
you're feeling jumpy." Marian shook her head, Mrs. Ericson watched
her dark, competent hands and wondered for the thousandth time how
the house had ever managed to get along without her, or how she had
lived through those earlier years when her household had been pre-
sided over by a series of slatternly white girls who had considered
housework demeaning and the care of the children an added insult.
"You drive beautifully, Marian," she said. "Now, don't think of the last
time. Anybody would slide down a steep hill on a wet day like that."

"It takes four mistakes to flunk you," Marian said. "I don't remem- 5
ber doing all the things the inspector marked down on my blank."

"People say that they only want you to slip them a little something," 6
Mrs. Ericson said doubtfully.

"*No*," Marian said. "That would only make it worse, Mrs. Ericson, I 7
know."

The car turned right, at a traffic signal, into a side road and slid up 8
to the curb at the rear of a short line of parked cars. The inspectors
had not arrived yet.

"You have the papers," Mrs. Ericson asked. Marian took them out 9
of her bag: her learner's permit, the car registration, and her birth
certificate. They settled down to the dreary business of waiting.

169

"It would be marvellous to have someone dependable to drive the   10
children to school every day," Mrs. Ericson said.

Marian looked up from the list of driving requirements she had
been studying. "It'll make things simpler at the house, won't it?" she
said.

"Oh, Marian," Mrs. Ericson exclaimed, "if I could only pay you half   11
of what you're worth!"

"Now, Mrs. Ericson," Marian said firmly. They looked at each   12
other and smiled with affection.

Two cars with official insignia on their doors stopped across the   13
street. The inspectors leaped out, very brisk and military in their neat
uniforms. Marian's hands tightened on the wheel. "There's the one
who flunked me last time," she whispered, pointing to a stocky, self-
important man who had begun to shout directions at the driver at the
head of the line. "Oh, Mrs. Ericson."

"Now, Marian," Mrs. Ericson said. They smiled at each other again,   14
rather weakly.

The inspector who finally reached their car was not the stocky one   15
but a genial, middle-aged man who grinned broadly as he thumbed
over their papers. Mrs. Ericson started to get out of the car. "Don't you
want to come along?" the inspector asked. "Mandy and I don't mind
company."

Mrs. Ericson was bewildered for a moment. "No," she said, and   16
stepped to the curb. "I might make Marian self-conscious. She's a fine
driver, Inspector."

"Sure thing," the inspector said, winking at Mrs. Ericson. He slid   17
into the seat beside Marian. "Turn right at the corner, Mandy-Lou."

From the curb, Mrs. Ericson watched the car move smoothly up the   18
street.

The inspector made notations in a small black book. "Age?" he in-   19
quired presently, as they drove along.

"Twenty-seven."   20

He looked at Marian out of the corner of his eye. "Old enough to   21
have quite a flock of pickaninnies, eh?"

Marian did not answer.   22

"Left at this corner," the inspector said, "and park between that   23
truck and the green Buick."

The two cars were very close together, but Marian squeezed in be-   24
tween them without too much maneuvering.

"Driven before, Mandy-Lou?" the inspector asked.   25

"Yes, sir. I had a license for three years in Pennsylvania."   26

"Why do you want to drive a car?"   27

"My employer needs me to take her children to and from school."   28

"Sure you don't really want to sneak out nights to meet some young   29
blood?" the inspector asked. He laughed as Marian shook her head.

"Let's see you take a left at the corner and then turn around in the   30
middle of the next block," the inspector said. He began to whistle
"Swanee River." "Make you homesick?" he asked.

Marian put out her hand, swung around neatly in the street, and   31
headed back in the direction from which they had come. "No," she
said. "I was born in Scranton, Pennsylvania."

The inspector feigned astonishment. "You-all ain't Southern?" he   32
said.

"Well, dog my cats if I didn't think you-all came from down yon-   33
dah."

"No, sir," Marian said.   34

"Turn onto Main Street and let's see how you-all does in heavier   35
traffic."

They followed a line of cars along Main Street for several blocks   36
until they came in sight of a concrete bridge which arched high over
the railroad tracks.

"Read that sign at the end of the bridge," the inspector said.   37

"'Proceed with caution. Dangerous in slippery weather,'" Marian   38
said.

"You-all sho can read fine," the inspector exclaimed. "Where d'you   39
learn to do that, Mandy?"

"I got my college degree last year," Marian said. Her voice was not   40
quite steady.

As the car crept up the slope of the bridge the inspector burst out   41
laughing. He laughed so hard he could scarcely give his next direction.
"Stop here," he said, wiping his eyes, "then start'er up again. Mandy
got her degree, did she? Dog my cats!"

Marian pulled up beside the curb. She put the car in neutral, pul-   42
led on the emergency, waited a moment, and then put the car in gear
again. Her face was set. As she released the brake her foot slipped off
the clutch pedal and the engine stalled.

"Now, Mistress Mandy," the inspector said, "remember your de-   43
gree."

"*Damn* you!" Marian cried. She started the car with a jerk.   44

The inspector lost his joviality in an instant. "Return to the starting   45
place, please," he said, and made four very black crosses at random in
the squares on Marian's application blank.

Mrs. Ericson was waiting at the curb where they had left her. As   46
Marian stopped the car, the inspector jumped out and brushed past
her, his face purple. "What happened?" Mrs. Ericson asked, looked
after him with alarm.

Marian stared down at the wheel and her lip trembled.   47

"Oh, Marian, *again*?" Mrs. Ericson said.   48

Marian nodded. "In a sort of different way," she said, and slid over   49
to the right-hand side of the car.

PART FIVE

Additional Readings

What's in a Name?

LOIS SWEET

It was parents' visiting day. A week before, we'd waved goodbye 1
to our 8-year-old daughter as she left on a bus for camp. We were
dying to see her again.

When we asked for her, we were told there wasn't anyone there by 2
that name. Our hearts stopped. What could have happened to her?

Well, said the counsellor, there wasn't anyone there by that *first* 3
name. There was a girl with that last name.

When we found her, she calmly announced that she'd changed her 4
name. No longer was she to be known by the name we'd given her at
birth—Dechinta. She had become Rachel, the girl of her middle name.

It may seem silly, but I take it seriously. Names are such state- 5
ments, such a form of self-identity, that any effort to change them has
to be considered.

Over the years, a lot of my friends have changed their names. A 6
number of them began to take an interest in their cultural backgrounds
and became horrified that their parents had Anglicized their names in
an effort to deny cultural differences. To my friends, being pushed
into the great bland melting pot felt more like being drowned than
saved. Their culture was a source of pride and they demanded recognition for their "ethnic" names.

Then there have been what seem like hundreds of friends whose 7
marriages ended. Having taken their husbands' names at marriage, deciding which name to use when they split up was a problem. Some
argued that reverting to their birth names would create professional
difficulties. After all, they'd established reputations based on their husbands' surnames.

Very Complicated

Others reclaimed their birth names, only to change again when 8
they remarried. It was very complicated. Whenever I wrote a letter to
one of them, I wasn't quite sure which name to put on the envelope.

A handful of friends changed their names when they discovered a 9
life cause. One person illustrated the seriousness of his newly found

174

conviction with a modified name change. No longer could we call him "Russ." He became "Russell" signifying that there was no room in the relationship for either casualness or false intimacy.

Still others chose to drop their last names completely in order to   10
flag their particular brand of radical feminism. Last names were a patriarchal remnant, they said, created to establish male ownership.

Although it takes a lot of effort to remember what to call whom, I   11
was among those who forced such an effort on others. When I got married 15 years ago, it never occurred to me not to take my husband's name. Ten years later, whose last name I was using became an issue.

I discovered that a married name is only an assumed name and   12
that reverting to my birth name involved neither lawyers nor bureaucracy. Although the name Sweet had been a plague during childhood, it did belong to me. I decided to reclaim it.

Open to Change
Everyone, except relatives, has been open to the change. Neverthe-   13
less, the step was worth it. It might have been an old name, but it characterized a new me.

So what does a name change mean for an 8-year-old? Probably that   14
the child recognizes that her name reveals more about her parents than about herself. The first name we gave our daughter (which, granted, is unusual, but not made up), is an Athapaskan Indian word meaning self-sufficiency. It says as much about our generation as the names Pearl or Thelma said about our parents'.

Several years ago, when our daughter's kindergarten teacher sent   15
home a class list, we were struck with how much that generation of children were stuck with the "counter-culture" influence. Moonbeam, Airborn and names like them were in the majority. It's the unfaddish, un-made-up Biblical names like Rachel, however, that wear like solid gold.

Changing names might be a bother for those who have to remem-   16
ber to use the new name, but it obviously has significance for the person who's insisting on the change. Rather than a new name bringing a new personality, I think a new name is a sign of a new personality—or at the very least, of a profound personality change.

A point not lost on countries, let alone people, is that the right to   17
name the world for yourself is a matter of great political importance.

If I can respect name changes in friends—and vice-versa—I can   18
respect it in my daughter. After all, families should be democratic.

I just hope it doesn't happen too often.   19

How Cocaine Took Control of My Life

TONY ELLIOTT

I was fortunate. Facing the barrel of a coke dealer's .357 Magnum revolver brought me to my senses and helped me realize that I needed help, that cocaine had taken control of my life. Len Bias and Don Rogers were not as lucky. They didn't get that kind of warning. 1

Let me share with you how this problem started for me. There were two related sources. First came the kinds of pressure that I faced as an athlete growing up in the inner city. 2

I grew up in Bridgeport, Conn., in a neighborhood where drug use was not looked down on by other kids and young adults. It was even seen as a means of rebelling. 3

I was using drugs and alcohol before I became an athlete at the age of 14. Being an athlete did not necessarily mean that drug use was over. Your prestige among your peers didn't diminish. In fact, I think my macho image was enhanced when people saw I was able to use and still perform as an athlete. Boozing it up is supposed to be a sign of manhood for the young athlete. Now it's coke, the champagne of drugs. It's a status symbol. It gives you the illusion of power and masculinity. It made me believe that nothing could happen to me. I'm sure Len Bias and Don Rogers felt the same way. 4

Like all high school athletes, I was asked to make sacrifices that other kids did not have to make. We were told to give up sex, partying and alcohol. I often felt that I was playing for the coach and not for myself. I found myself trying to get away with as much as I could. Avoid the exercise and drills if the coaches weren't watching. Stay up as late as you could. Drink and use drugs if you could get away with it. I got away with it. 5

As a young adolescent, I had difficulty trying to confirm my sense of identity. I desperately needed to be accepted. I always wondered if I was liked only because I was a football star or because I had drugs to pass around. The delusions are easy to build up but painful to take down. 6

As a star high school athlete, there were plenty of pressures that 7
went along with the attention. I often felt that the reputation of our
entire school was being carried on my shoulders as I played each game.
Was I going to be a hero this week or a zero? Drugs and alcohol were a
welcome relief from this pressure from the coaches, schoolmates, the
community and, most of all, from myself. I used drugs in response to
sports success. The thrill of victory in competition, for me, is a natural
high. I experienced the same euphoric feeling from cocaine that I felt
during game conditions. Therefore, as an athlete, I feel that I was
more susceptible to cocaine addiction than the average person. I feel
that many athletes are. Those who have never tried it are very fortunate because after a while it is no longer enjoyable. It was like a demon
in me that made life miserable as I constantly sought that euphoric
feeling that was never there.

The second set of reasons for my drug use came from the fact that 8
as an athlete, all authority figures systematically removed responsibility
from me off the field. I had fewer chores, I had to study less, I got
away with more in school, I never had to make plans. Everything was
done for me. All I had to do was play the game. This made it difficult
for me to accept responsibility for my own behavior. They were wrong
for doing this and I was wrong for allowing it to happen, but in the end
I was the one who almost died.

I knew that my grades in school were directly related to my per- 9
formance on the field. If I played better, I could study even less. I
began to understand the rules of the game.

In college, the system became even more exaggerated. I was given 10
money, apartments, cars. I didn't have to do anything but play ball.
Nobody doubted my intelligence. But nobody asked me to study. I was
a football star.

I was heavily into drug use by my senior year, 1981. I *knew* I was 11
invincible the next spring when I was drafted and signed by the New
Orleans Saints. Not only was I signed but I got a $30,000 signing bo-
nus!

As a professional, when the athlete returns to his community the 12
easiest way to keep ties with his former associates and to assure him
that he has not forgotten "where he came from" is to use drugs or
share his earnings with his friends by treating them to drugs. I spent
the $30,000 in a two-week cocaine binge in my hometown.

Over a four-year period, I believe I spent close to a million dollars 13
on cocaine for me and my friends. I sold everything I had, ruined my
first marriage, became a petty criminal, and finally peered down the
barrel of my own personal Grim Reaper. Desperate, I had planned to
hold up my dealer with a cheap pistol, but when the door opened I was
on the other side of a .357 Magnum. At that time, a light went on and I
was saved.

Yet I can see how Len Bias and Don Rogers didn't recognize the   14
imminence of their own "suicides." One night I sat alone with a pipe.
There was a little bit of coke left when I began to feel sharp chest
pains. I knew I was in trouble yet I chose to take that last hit and not
deal with my heart. That's how powerful the stuff is. It's so powerful
that Don Rogers took a dose just days after Bias's death. The ultimate
tragedy of their deaths will be if we, as athletes and as a society, treat
their deaths as isolated incidents. With millions of high school athletes
abusing chemicals and alcohol, we are facing a monster near victory.
Drug testing might help but it isn't the key. Education is. If the deaths
of two physically gifted men at the top of their games doesn't scare us
enough to make us see the monster eating our souls, what will?

I wish I knew the answer. I do know we have to be able to see that   15
it is a monster and that we are all its potential prey.

Note: Tony Elliott was allowed back into the National Football League
in November 1984 as a result of his work speaking with young children
on the subject of drug abuse.

Television: The Plug-in Drug

MARIE WINN

Real People

It is not only the activities that a family might engage in together 1
that are diminished by the powerful presence of television in the home.
The relationships of the family members to each other are also affected, in both obvious and subtle ways. The hours that the young child
spends in a one-way relationship with television people, an involvement
that allows for no communication or interaction, surely affect his relationships with real-life people.

Studies show the importance of eye-to-eye contact, for instance, in 2
real-life relationships, and indicate that the nature of a person's eye-
contact patterns, whether he looks another squarely in the eye or looks
to the side or shifts his gaze from side to side, may play a significant
role in his success or failure in human relationships. But no eye contact
is possible in the child-television relationship, although in certain children's programs people purport to speak directly to the child and the
camera fosters this illusion by focusing directly upon the person being
filmed. (Mr. Rogers is an example, telling the child "I like you, you're
special," etc.) How might such a distortion of real-life relationships affect a child's development of trust, of openness, of an ability to relate
well to the *real* people?

Bruno Bettelheim writes: 3

> Children who have been taught, or conditioned, to listen passively
> most of the day to the warm verbal communications coming from the
> TV screen, to the deep emotional appeal of the so-called TV person-
> ality, are often unable to respond to real persons because they arouse
> so much less feeling than the skilled actor. Worse, they lose the ability
> to learn from reality because life experiences are much more compli-
> cated than the ones they see on the screen. . . .

A teacher makes a similar observation about her personal viewing 4
experiences:

"I have trouble mobilizing myself and dealing with real people af- 5

179

ter watching a few hours of television. It's just hard to make that transition from watching television to a real relationship. I suppose it's because there was no effort necessary while I was watching, and dealing with real people always requires a bit of effort. Imagine, then, how much harder it might be to do the same thing for a small child, particularly one who watches a lot of television every day."

But more obviously damaging to family relationships is the elimina-   6
tion of opportunities to talk, and perhaps more important, to argue, to air grievances, between parents and children and brothers and sisters. Families frequently use television to avoid confronting their problems, problems that will not go away if they are ignored but will only fester and become less easily resolvable as time goes on.

A mother reports: 7

"I find myself, with three children, wanting to turn on the TV set   8
when they're fighting. I really have to struggle not to do it because I feel that's telling them this is the solution to the quarrel—but it's so tempting that I often do it."

A family therapist discusses the use of television as an avoidance   9
mechanism:

"In a family I know the father comes home from work and turns   10
on the television set. The children come and watch with him and the wife serves them their meal in front of the set. He then goes and takes a shower, or works on the car or something. She then goes and has her own dinner in front of the television set. It's a symptom of a deeper-rooted problem, sure. But it would help them all to get rid of the set. It would be far easier to work on what the symptom really means without the television. The television simply encourages a double avoidance of each other. They'd find out more quickly what was going on if they weren't able to hide behind the TV. Things wouldn't necessarily be better, of course, but they wouldn't be anesthetized."

The decreased opportunities for simple conversation between par-   11
ents and children in the television-centered home may help explain an observation made by an emergency room nurse at a Boston hospital. She reports that parents just seem to sit there these days when they come in with a sick or seriously injured child, although talking to the child would distract and comfort him. "They don't seem to know *how* to talk to their own children at any length," the nurse observes. Similarly, a television critic writes in *The New York Times:* "I had just a day ago taken my son to the emergency ward of a hospital for stitches above his left eye, and the occasion seemed no more real to me than Maalot or 54th Street, south-central Los Angeles. There was distance and numbness and an inability to turn off the total institution. I didn't behave at all; I just watched. . . .

A number of research studies substantiate the assumption that tele-   12

vision interferes with family activities and the formation of family relationships. One survey shows that 78 percent of the respondents indicated no conversation taking place during viewing except at specified
times such as commercials. The study notes: "The television atmosphere in most households is one of quiet absorption on the part of
family members who are present. The nature of the family social life
during a program could be described as 'parallel' rather than interac-
tive, and the set does seem to dominate family life when it is on."
Thirty-six percent of the respondents in another study indicated that
television viewing was the only family activity participated in during the
week.

In a summary of research findings on television's effect on family 13
interactions James Gabardino states: "The early findings suggest that
television had a disruptive effect upon interaction and thus presumably
human development. . . . It is not unreasonable to ask: 'Is the fact that
the average American family during the 1950s came to include two
parents, two children and a television set somehow related to the psy-
chosocial characteristics of the young adults of the 1970s?'"

Undermining the Family

In its effect on family relationships, in its facilitation of parental 14
withdrawal from an active role in the socialization of their children,
and in its replacement of family rituals and special events, television
has played an important role in the disintegration of the American
family. But of course it has not been the only contributing factor, perhaps not even the most important one. The steadily rising divorce rate,
the increase in the number of working mothers, the decline of the ex-
tended family, the breakdown of neighborhoods and communities, the
growing isolation of the nuclear family—all have seriously affected the
family.

As Urie Bronfenbrenner suggests, the sources of family breakdown 15
do not come from the family itself, but from the circumstances in
which the family finds itself and the way of life imposed upon it by
those circumstances. "When those circumstances and the way of life
they generate undermine relationships of trust and emotional security
between family members, when they make it difficult for parents to
care for, educate and enjoy their children, when there is no support or
recognition from the outside world for one's role as a parent and when
time spent with one's family means frustration of career, personal ful-
fillment and peace of mind, then the development of the child is adver-
sely affected," he writes.

But while the roots of alienation go deep into the fabric of Ameri- 16
can social history, television's presence in the home fertilizes them, encourages their wild and unchecked growth. Perhaps it is true that

America's commitment to the television experience masks a spiritual vacuum, an empty and barren way of life, a desert of materialism. But it is television's dominant role in the family that anesthetizes the family into accepting its unhappy state and prevents it from struggling to better its condition, to improve its relationships, and to regain some of the richness it once possessed.

Others have noted the role of mass media in perpetuating an un-   17
satisfactory *status quo*. Leisure-time activity, writes Irving Howe, "must provide relief from work monotony without making the return to work too unbearable; it must provide amusement without insight and pleasure without disturbance—as distinct from art which gives pleasure through disturbance. Mass culture is thus oriented towards a central aspect of industrial society: the depersonalization of the individual." Similarly, Jacques Ellul rejects the idea that television is a legitimate means of educating the citizen: "Education . . . takes place only incidentally. The clouding of his consciousness is paramount. . . ."

And so the American family muddles on, dimly aware that some-   18
thing is amiss but distracted from an understanding of its plight by an endless stream of television images. As family ties grow weaker and vaguer, as children's lives become more separate from their parents', as parents' educational role in their children's lives is taken over by television and schools, family life becomes increasingly more unsatisfying for both parents and children. All that seems to be left is Love, an abstraction that family members *know* is necessary but find great difficulty giving each other because the traditional opportunities for expressing love within the family have been reduced or destroyed.

For contemporary parents, love toward each other has increasingly   19
come to mean successful sexual relations, as witnessed by the proliferation of sex manuals and sex therapists. The opportunities for manifesting other forms of love through mutual support, understanding, nurturing, even, to use an unpopular word, *serving* each other, are less and less available as mothers and fathers seek their independent destinies outside the family.

As for love of children, this love is increasingly expressed through   20
supplying material comforts, amusements, and educational opportunities. Parents show their love for their children by sending them to good schools and camps, by providing them with good food and good doctors, by buying them toys, books, games, and a television set of their very own. Parents will even go further and express their love by attending PTA meetings to improve their children's schools, or by joining groups that are acting to improve the quality of their children's television programs.

But this is love at a remove, and is rarely understood by children.   21
The more direct forms of parental love require time and patience,

steady, dependable, ungrudgingly given time actually spent *with* a child, reading to him, comforting him, playing, joking, and working with him. But even if a parent were eager and willing to demonstrate that sort of direct love to his children today, the opportunities are diminished. What with school and Little League and piano lessons and, of course, the inevitable television programs, a day seems to offer just enough time for a good-night kiss.

Punishment versus Discipline

BRUNO BETTELHEIM

A parent who respects himself will feel no need to demand or command respect from his child, since he feels no need for the child's respect to buttress his security as a parent or as a person. Secure in himself, he will not feel his authority threatened and will accept it when his child sometimes shows a lack of respect for him, as young children, in particular, are apt to do. The parent's self-respect tells him that such displays arise from immaturity of judgment, which time and experience will eventually correct.

Demanding or commanding respect reveals to the child an insecure parent who lacks the conviction that his way of life will, all by itself, over time, gain him the child's respect. Not trusting that respect will come naturally, this parent has to insist on it right now. Who would wish to form himself in the image of an insecure person, even if that person is his parent? Unfortunately, the child of insecure parents often becomes an insecure person himself, because insecure parents cannot inculcate security in their children or create an environment in which the children can develop a sense of security on their own.

To be disciplined requires self-control. To be controlled by others and to accept living by their rules or orders makes it superfluous to control oneself. When the more important aspects of a child's actions and behavior are controlled by, say, his parents or teachers, he will see no need to learn to control himself; others do it for him.

How parents in other cultures try to inculcate self-control in their children can be instructive. Consider, for example, a study designed to find out why young Japanese do much better academically than Americans. When the researchers studied maternal behavior they saw clear differences between the Japanese and the Americans. Typically, when young American children ran around in supermarkets, their mothers—often annoyed—told them, "Stop that!" or "I told you not to act this way!" Japanese mothers typically refrained entirely from telling their children what to do. Instead they asked them questions, such as "How do you think it makes the storekeeper feel when you run around like this in his store?" or "How do you think it makes me feel when my child runs around as you do?" Similarly, the American mother, wanting her child to eat what he was supposed to eat, would order the child to do so or tell him that he ought to eat it because it was good for him. The Japanese mother would ask her child a question, such as "How do you think it makes the man who grew these vegetables for you to eat feel when you reject them?" or "How do you think it makes these carrots that grew so that you could eat them feel when you do not eat them?" Thus from a very early age the American child is told what to do, while the Japanese child is encouraged not only to consider other persons' feelings but to control himself on the basis of his own deliberations.

The reason for the higher academic achievement of Japanese 5 youngsters may well be that the Japanese child in situations important to his mother is invited to think things out on his own, a habit that stands him in good stead when he has to master academic material. The American child, in contrast, is expected to conform his decisions and actions to what he is told to do. This expectation certainly does not encourage him to do his own thinking.

The Japanese mother does not just expect her child to be able to 6 arrive at good decisions. She also makes an appeal to her child not to embarrass her. In the traditional Japanese culture losing face is among the worst things that can happen to a person. When a mother asks, "How do you think it makes me—or the storekeeper—feel when you act this way?" she implies that by mending his ways the child does her, or the storekeeper, a very great favor. To be asked to do one's own thinking and to act accordingly, as well as to be told that one is able to do someone a favor, enhances one's self-respect, while to be ordered to do the opposite of what one wants is destructive of it.

What is a parent to do in the short run to prevent a child from 7 misbehaving, as children are apt to do from time to time? Ideally, letting a child know of our disappointment should be effective and should lead the child to abstain from repeating the wrongdoing in the future. Realistically, even if a child has great love and respect for us, his parents, simply telling him of our disappointment, or showing him how great it is, will not always suffice to remedy the situation.

When our words are not enough, when telling our child to mend 8 his ways is ineffective, then the threat of the withdrawal of our love and affection is the only sound method to impress on him that he had better conform to our request. Subconsciously recognizing how powerful a threat this is, some parents, with the best of intentions, destroy its effectiveness by assuring their children that they love them no matter what. This might well be true, but it does not sound convincing to a child, who knows that he does not love his parents no matter what, such as when they are angry at him; so how can he believe them when he can tell that they are dissatisfied, and maybe even angry at him? Most of us do not really love unconditionally. Therefore any effort to make ourselves look better, to pretend to be more loving than we are, will have the opposite effect from the one we desire. True, our love for our child can be so deep, so firmly anchored in us, that it will withstand even very severe blows. But at the moment when we are seriously disappointed in the child, our love may be at a low point, and if we want the child to change his ways, he might as well know it.

The action to take is to banish the child from our presence. We 9 may send him out of the room or we ourselves may withdraw. Whatever, the parent is clearly indicating, "I am so disappointed in you that I do not wish, or feel unable, to maintain physical closeness with you." Here physical distance stands for emotional distance, and it is a symbol that speaks to the child's conscious and unconscious at the same time. This is why the action is so effective.

Sending the child out of sight permits both parent and child to 10 gain distance from what has happened, to cool off, to reconsider. And that does help. But it is the threat of desertion, as likely as not, that permanently impresses the child. Separation anxiety is probably the earliest and most basic anxiety of man. The infant experiences it when his prime caretaker absents herself from him, an absence that, should it become permanent and the caretaker not be replaced, would indeed lead to the infant's death. Anything that rekindles this anxiety is experienced as a terrible threat. Hence, as long as a child believes, however vaguely, that his very existence is in danger if his prime caretaker deserts him, he will respond to this real, implied, or imagined threat with deep feelings of anxiety. Even when he is old enough to know that his life is not in real danger, he will respond to separation from a parent with severe feelings of dejection, because to some degree he will feel as if he were endangered. The difference is that at an older age the fear is not of physical but of emotional starvation.

If we should have any doubt that physical separation can be an 11 effective expression of our disgust with a child's behavior, we can look to our children themselves to set us straight. The worst that a child can think of when he is disgusted with his parents is that he will run away. He makes such a threat because he is convinced that it is so terrible that it will compel us to mend our ways. Clearly, a child understands very well that when we threaten to distance ourselves from him physically we are threatening to distance ourselves from him emotionally. That threat makes a very deep impression.

We must be honest about our strong emotional reactions to our 12 children's behavior, showing our children how deeply we love them, on the one hand, and, on the other, letting them know when we are disappointed in them, provided we do not become critical or punitive. This is all just part of being ourselves. We need not make any claim to be perfect. But if we strive as best we can to live good lives ourselves, our children, impressed by the merits of living good lives, will one day wish to do the same.

The Mirages of Marriage

WILLIAM J. LEDERER
DONALD D. JACKSON

The offices of marriage counselors, psychologists, and psychiatrists are crowded with clients who are concerned over problems which mainly involve marriage, and who pay from twenty-five dollars to fifty dollars an hour for assistance. But these troubled people usually cannot identify their problems; even worse, they usually do not sincerely seek solutions. What each one wants is confirmation that he is correct and good, and that his spouse is the one at fault!

One reason for this marital disenchantment is the prevalence of the mistaken belief that "love" is necessary for a satisfying and workable marriage. Usually when the word "love" is used, reference is actually being made to romance—that hypnotic, ecstatic condition enjoyed during courtship. Romance and love are different. Romance is based usually on minimum knowledge of the other person (restricted frequently to the fact that being around him is a wonderful, beatific, stimulating experience). Romance is built on a foundation of quicksilver nonlogic. It consists of attributing to the other person—blindly, hopefully, but without much basis in fact—the qualities one *wishes* him to have, though they may not even be desirable, in actuality. Most people who select mates on the basis of imputed qualities later find themselves disappointed, if the qualities are not present in fact, or discover that they are unable to tolerate the implication of the longed-for qualities in actual life. For example, the man who is attracted by his fiancée's cuteness and sexiness may spend tormented hours after they are married worrying about the effect of these very characteristics on other men. It is a dream relationship, an unrealistic relationship with a dream person imagined in terms of one's own needs.

Romance is essentially selfish, though it is expressed in terms of glittering sentiment and generous promises, which usually cannot be fulfilled. ("I'll be the happiest man in the world of the rest of my life." "I'll make you the best wife any man ever had.")

Romance—*which most spouses mistake for love*—is not necessary for a

good marriage. The sparkle some couples manage to preserve in a satisfying marriage—based on genuine pleasure in one another's company, affection and sexual attraction for the spouse as he really is—can
be called love.

If romance is different than love, then what *is* love? We do best to   5
return to the definition of Harry Stack Sullivan: "When the satisfaction
or the security of another person becomes as significant to one as is
one's own satisfaction or security, then the state of love exists." In this
sense, love consists of a devotion and respect for the spouse that is
equal to one's own self-love.

We have already shown that people usually marry on a wave of   6
romance having nothing to do with love. When the average American
(not long from the altar) lives with the spouse in the intimacy of morning bad breath from too much smoking, of annoying habits previously
not known, when he is hampered by the limitations of a small income
(compared with the lavishness of the honeymoon), or encounters the
unexpected irritability of premenstrual tension or of business frustration and fatigue, a change in attitude begins to occur. The previously
romantic person begins to have doubts about the wonderful attributes
with which his spouse has been so blindly credited.

These doubts are particularly disturbing at the start. Not very long   7
ago, after all, the spouse believed that "love" (romance) was heavenly,
all-consuming, immutable, and that beautiful relationships and behavior were *voluntary* and *spontaneous*. Now, if doubts and criticism are per-
mitted to intrude upon this perfect dream, the foundations begin to
shake in a giddy manner. To the husband or wife the doubts seem to
be evidence that one of them is inadequate or not to be trusted. The
doubts imply that the relationship is suffering from an unsuspected
malignancy.

To live with another person in a state of love (as defined by Sul-   8
livan) is a different experience from whirling around in a tornado of
romance. A loving union is perhaps best seen in elderly couples who
have been married for a long time. Their children have grown, the
pressure of business has been relieved, and the specter of death is not
far away. But now, they have achieved a set of realistic values. These
elderly spouses respect each other's idiosyncrasies. They need and trea-
sure companionship. Differences between them have been either accepted or worked out; they are no longer destructive elements. In such
instances each has as much interest in the well-being and security of the
other as he has in himself. Here is true symbiosis: a union where each
admittedly feeds off the other. Those who give together really live together!

The Pursuit of Loneliness

PHILIP SLATER

The Great Illusion

It's easy to produce examples of the many ways in which Ameri- 1
cans try to minimize, circumvent, or deny the interdependence upon
which all human societies are based. We seek a private house, a private
means of transportation, a private garden, a private laundry, self-serv-
ice stores, and do-it-yourself skills of every kind. An enormous technology seems to have set itself the task of making it unnecessary for one
human being ever to ask anything of another in the course of going
about his or her daily business. Even within the family Americans are
unique in their feeling that each member should have a separate room,
and even a separate telephone, television, and car, when economically
possible. We seek more and more privacy, and feel more and more
alienated and lonely when we get it. And what accidental contacts we
do have seem more intrusive, not only because they're unsought, but
because they're not connected with any familiar pattern of interdependence.

Most important, our encounters with others tend increasingly to be 2
competitive as we search for more privacy. We less and less often meet
our fellow humans to share and exchange, and more and more often
encounter them as an impediment or a nuisance: making the highway
crowded when we're rushing somewhere, cluttering and littering the
beach or park or wood, pushing in front of us at the supermarket,
taking the last parking place, polluting our air and water, building a
highway through our house, blocking our view, and so on. Because
we've cut off so much communication with each other we keep bump-
ing into each other, so that a higher and higher percentage of our
interpersonal contacts are abrasive.

We seem unable to foresee that the gratification of a wish might 3
turn out to be a monkey's paw if the wish were shared by many others.
We cheer the new road that shaves ten minutes off the drive to our
country retreat but ultimately transforms it into a crowded resort and
increases both the traffic and the time. We're continually surprised to

190

find, when we want something, that thousands or millions of others want it, too—that other human beings get hot in summer and cold in winter. The worst traffic jams occur when a mass of vacationing tourist start home early to "beat the traffic." We're too enamored of the individualistic fantasy that everyone is, or should be, different—that a man could somehow build his entire life around some single eccentricity without boring himself and everyone else to death. We all have our quirks, which provide surface variety, but aside from this, human beings have little basis for their persistent claim that they are not all members of the same species.

The Freedom Fix

Since our contacts with others are increasingly competitive, unanticipated, and abrasive, we seek still more apartness and thus accelerate the trend. The desire to be somehow special sparks an even more competitive quest for progressively more rare and expensive symbols—a quest that is ultimately futile since it is individualism itself that produces uniformity. 4

This is poorly understood by Americans, who tend to confuse uniformity with "conformity," in the sense of compliance with group demands. Many societies exert far more pressure on the individual to mold herself to play a sharply defined role in a total group pattern, but there is variation among these circumscribed roles. Our society gives more leeway to the individual to pursue her own ends, but since the culture defines what is worthy and desirable, everyone tends, independently but monotonously, to pursue the same things in the same way. Thus cooperation tends to produce variety, while competition generates uniformity. 5

The problem with individualism is not that it is immoral but that it is incorrect. The universe does not consist of a lot of unrelated particles but is an interconnected whole. Pretending that our fortunes are independent of each other may be perfectly ethical, but it's also perfectly stupid. Individualistic thinking is unflagging in the production of false dichotomies, such as "conformity *vs.* independence," "altruism *vs.* egoism," "inner-directed *vs.* other-directed," and so on, all of which are built upon the absurd assumption that the individual can be considered separately from the environment of which he or she is a part. 6

A favorite delusion of individualism—one that it attempts, through education and propaganda, to make real—is that only egoistic responses are spontaneous. But this is not so: collective responses—helping behavior, nurturance, supportiveness, the assumption of specialized roles in group tasks, rituals, or games—these are natural, not trained, even among animals. People are more *self-consciously* oriented toward others in competitive, individualistic societies—their behavior is calcu- 7 lated. They accommodate to others because they want to look good, impress people, protect themselves from shame and guilt, and avoid confronting people directly. In more organic and cooperative communities people respond spontaneously to impulses that are neither selfish nor unselfish, but more directly from the heart. Sometimes they look generous, sometimes grasping, but what's important is that the behavior is *to* others, not an effort to produce some sort of *effect* on others. Cooperative societies are unassuming—it's the competitive ones that are concerned with appearances.

Males Just Born Gross—Humor Them

STEPHANIE BRUSH

Dr. Frank Hurley of Research Triangle Park, N.C., has written 1
to me about an important subject: male grossness. His comments are
based on a column I wrote a few months back, about men de-evolving
to a primitive state when left alone by the womenfolk over the weekend.

"We males are naturally crude, a gift females do not have," he 2
writes insightfully. "And the quality of crudeness is not strained, nor
can it be cultivated." (Where was this man when the Supreme Court
nominees were being considered?)

Dr. Hurley cites the inability of women to tell gross jokes prop- 3
erly—they are often "physically unable" to say the punch line, no matter how much their hearts may desire to. It's been my observation that
we often degenerate into weak hand gestures, impotent giggling, silly
blushing, and worse.

I think that it is important for a man to take women to task for 4
their failure to be truly gross. What can we do but throw up our hands
and claim shameful defeat? Ever since Jimmy Mangiamelli chased me
around the coat closet waving the body parts of a small, dead hamster
at me in the third grade, I have recognized the inalienable right of
human males to be gross.

This may take the form of belching competitions, scab-excavation, 5
bathroom humor, and misuse of normal body functions, in general.

I have recently noticed a grossly strange entertainment/grooming 6
trend among young males on both coasts of the United States, and I
am wondering if it can be a coincidence: while I was sitting in a park in
Seattle recently, a man came up to me wearing what appeared to be a
rubber dog nose and tried to make friends with me.

"It is difficult for me to cozy up to strangers in general, not to 7
mention strangers wearing rubber dog noses," I said to him politely.
And he seemed crestfallen. (Gross, but crestfallen.)

193

Later, on the East Coast

Then, about a week later, I was in a parking lot in Connecticut, and 8
three or four young men came running past in a larky, exuberant fashion, wearing rubber *pig* noses. I acted as if men wearing rubber pig noses was a fairly regular phenomenon in coastal Connecticut, and they, too, seemed crestfallen. The reaction from women that they had sought ("OH GROSS!!") had been registered in other quarters, but *I* had sorely let them down.

Lately, I seem to be surrounded by aggressively escalating levels of 9
male grossness. My half-brother, Doug, is entering the winsome phase of grossness that accompanies puberty: the strange desire to attract women (he discusses comparative hairstyling products with his male friends), and at the same time make them shriek in horror.

Poison Ivy Competition

The other day I ran into Doug, and he had a case of poison ivy on 10
his legs that looked like something a special-effects technician from a horror movie might have tried, and discarded, on the grounds of obscenity. Doug was proud of it—that's the thing. Pretty soon, his friend Larry came running up, and Larry had an identical case of poison ivy on *his* legs.

So it was clear that they had engaged in a gross-out contest. The 11
winner was the one who could make frail women faint dead away.

Do I understand the Grossness Imperative? Not a bit. Actually, I 12
do not understand testosterone as a concept, and never have—particularly the strange habits it engenders, whether it is wearing animal face masks or drinking enough beer to kill a sizable jungle animal, or annexing most of the Middle East, as a Growth Experience.

Actually, I like the fact that men are men. I would say, *"Vive la 13
difference"*—but that's a French expression. And I ask you: What would the civilization that invented headwaiters and crumb pushers know about grossness?

The Darkness After

ED AND LORRAINE WARREN WITH ROBERT DAVID CHASE

Maybe it was her breath, Mandy Robison thought to herself. 1
Maybe it was bad and she didn't even know it.

Or maybe it was the new perfume she was using. 2

Whatever it was, her sudden lack of popularity with her friends in 3
eleventh grade was getting hard to explain.

Here was a pretty and friendly sixteen-year-old who only two 4
weeks earlier had been one of the most popular girls in her class and
then—

Then her boyfriend of eleven months suddenly broke up with her. 5

Then her manager at the McDonald's where she worked after 6
school decided to take her from the counter and stick her in the back
where nobody could see her.

As if he were ashamed of her or something. 7

So what was it? Bad breath? The wrong perfume? A sudden case of 8
leprosy that she was the last to know about?

At this point, Mandy made no connection between the books she'd 9
been reading lately and the sudden downturn in her social fortunes.

But a quick glance at her bookcase showed her to have most pecu- 10
liar reading tastes.

On the first shelf you found such titles as *The Compleat Warlock;* 11
Satan Is My Friend; and *My Nights with Demons.* To say nothing of the
second shelf, which included such masterpieces as: *Contacting the Other
Realm; Fifteen Weeks in Hell;* and *Knowing the Darkness.*

During a baby-sitting job the past summer, Mandy had started 12
reading whatever paperbacks the Folsoms had lying around their
somewhat messy house. The Folsoms had seemed to have a genuine
interest in occult matters, hence all these really weird books on other
worlds beyond our own.

The thing was, Mandy took these tomes largely as jokes. She loved 13
to leaf through them, stumble upon some incantation that would sup-
posedly open the gates of hell, and then speak the incantation aloud

until she found herself laughing so hard that tears rolled down her cheeks.

Good clean harmless fun.   14

But then all of a sudden her friends started finding reasons to not   15
be her friends anymore.

What was going on here?   16

"There was just something about her. I'm not even sure I can ex-   17
plain it," a young man named Roland Klever explains to the inter-
viewer. "Here she was, this really cute girl that most of the boys really
wanted to date, but then something changed about her.

"I remember seeing her going down the hall one day and there was   18
this very dark aura around her. It shone on her face and made her
look like this real old hag. But when you'd blink the aura would be
gone and Mandy would be her old self again.

"I wasn't the only one who saw it. Her boyfriend Jack saw it too.   19
That's why he broke up with her. He really got afraid. People were
whispering about her all the time but she didn't seem to catch on."

Cathy Miles, a bright, attractive woman who was once Mandy's best   20
friend, later revealed: "I was out for an after-school walk with Mandy
one day and I saw her change shape. Literally. She became this demon.
I didn't scream—I was afraid I was losing my mind or hallucinating
and I figured that if I screamed, that would only call attention to my
problem. But then I started talking to other kids—and they started
seeing strange things happening around Mandy too."

Mandy first became aware of her difficulty when she was walking   21
home with a nine-year-old boy named Clint trailing behind her.

Clint had had a terrible crush on Mandy for the past year. He   22
often asked Mandy if she believed in younger men and older women
having affairs. Mandy always smiled to herself and said no.

On her way home from school one afternoon, Clint riding several   23
feet behind her on his Schwinn, Mandy turned to face the boy—only to
watch him scream like somebody in a sci-fi movie who'd just seen a
monster.

He started pedaling back the way he'd come, obviously afraid to   24
even turn around.

Stunned, and suspicious, Mandy stood staring after the boy for sev-   25
eral long minutes.

She thought of how strangely other people had been acting, too.   26

What was going on here, anyway?   27

She walked on home.   28

That night, when she was daubing some Clearasil on a zit, she fi-   29 nally realized why all her friends—and even lovesick Clint—had been acting so peculiarly around her.

That night, in the mirror, she saw the old hag the others 30 glimpsed—pus running from sores that looked like moon craters, red eyes that cast an eerie glow, teeth that were no more than blackened stubs, and warts that turned outward at odd and disgusting angles.

When her parents found her, she was lying naked on the bathroom 31 floor, sobbing and screaming and rolling back and forth as if in the power of some invisible force.

How to Stay Alive

ART HOPPE

O nce upon a time there was a man named Snadley Klab- 1
berhorn who was the healthiest man in the whole wide world.

Snadley wasn't always the healthiest man in the whole wide world. 2
When he was young, Snadley smoked what he wanted, drank what he
wanted, ate what he wanted, and exercised only with young ladies in
bed.

He thought he was happy. "Life is absolutely peachy," he was fond 3
of saying. "Nothing beats being alive."

Then along came the Surgeon General's Report linking smoking to 4
lung cancer, heart disease, emphysema, and tertiary coreopsis.

Snadley read about The Great Tobacco Scare with a frown. "Life is 5
so peachy," he said, "that there's no sense taking any risks." So he gave
up smoking.

Like most people who went through the hell of giving up smoking, 6
Snadley became more interested in his own health. In fact, he became
fascinated. And when he read a WCTU tract which pointed out that
alcohol caused liver damage, brain damage, and acute *weltanschauung*,
he gave up alcohol and drank dietary colas instead.

At least he did until The Great Cyclamate Scare. 7

"There's no sense in taking any risks," he said. And he switched to 8
sugar-sweetened colas, which made him fat and caused dental caries.
On realizing this he renounced colas in favor of milk and took up jogging, which was an awful bore.

That was about the time of The Great Cholesterol Scare. 9

Snadley gave up milk. To avoid cholesterol, which caused ath- 10
erosclerosis, coronary infarcts, and chronic chryselephantinism, he also
gave up meat, fats, and dairy products, subsisting on a diet of raw fish.

Then came The Great DDT Scare. 11

"The presence of large amounts of DDT in fish . . ." Snadley read 12
with anguish. But fortunately that's when he met Ernestine. They were
made for each other. Ernestine introduced him to homeground wheat
germ, macrobiotic yogurt, and organic succotash.

They were very happy eating this dish twice daily, watching six 13

198

hours of color television together and spending the rest of their time in bed.

They were, that is, until The Great Color Television Scare. 14

"If color tee-vee does give off radiations," said Snadley, "there's no 15 sense taking risks. After all, we still have each other."

And that's about all they had. Until The Great Pill Scare. 16

On hearing that The Pill might cause carcinoma, thromboses, and 17 lingering stichometry, Ernestine promptly gave up The Pill—and Snadley. "There's no sense taking any risks," she said.

Snadley was left with jogging. He was, that is, until he read some- 18 where that 1.3 percent of joggers are eventually run over by a truck or bitten by rabid dogs.

He then retired to a bomb shelter in his back yard (to avoid being 19 hit by a meteor), installed an air purifier (after The Great Smog Scare), and spent the next 63 years doing Royal Canadian Air Force exercises and poring over back issues of *The Reader's Digest*.

"Nothing's more important than being alive," he said proudly on 20 reaching 102. But he never did say anymore that life was absolutely peachy.

The Monsters in My Head

FRANK LANGELLA

I was sure he was coming to get me. First a hard step on the gravel and then a foot dragging behind. Step-drag, step-drag. I lay frozen in my bed. The long alleyway between our family house and the neighbor's was hardly three feet wide; dark, covered with black dirt, gravel and tufts of weeds and grass just barely able to survive the sunless space. The two windows of my room faced the clapboard wall of our neighbor's house, and Venetian blinds remained permanently closed against the nonview.

It was the mid-1940's. I had just seen a movie about a mummy. I don't remember the name of it. Just the image, so powerful even still, of a man wrapped in grayish cloth around his ankles, legs, body up to the top of his head. Eyes and mouth exposed, one arm drawn up against his chest, elbow close to his side, hand clawed. The other arm dangling alongside the leg that dragged. Several strips of cloth hung loosely from that arm, swaying with each step-drag, step-drag. I don't remember where he was coming from or going to in the movie. It doesn't really matter. I knew that he was coming for me.

For so many nights I heard him as I lay alone in my bed. My heart pounded as I waited for the good foot to land. A pause, then the slow drag. I would get up from the bed, pull the blind as little as I could away from the glass; and, with my chin just a little over the window ledge, I would stare hard into the dark alley. There were no outdoor lights, so I never could see him clearly. But he was there. He stopped when he saw me. I would get back into bed and wait. He usually left. Sometimes I fell asleep, and he returned, waking me. Other nights, he spared me and moved on.

I never told anyone about him. I don't know why. Shame, I suppose. It was that he seemed to be my private terror, and as much as I was frightened of him, I was also frightened of losing him. One night, he deserted me forever, and I was not to think of him again for 40 years, until my own son, this year, at age 4, began calling out in the night: "Daddy, daddy! There's a monster in my room. Come kill him." His room, several floors above the street, looks out over a New York

alleyway to a brick wall. The windows are covered with louvered shut-
ters. I found him sitting up in bed, eyes wide, staring at the tilted
louvers, pointing at his monster. "He's coming in the window, daddy.
He's going to get me."

I grabbed a pillow and did a dutiful daddy fight with the monster,   5
backing him up against the closet door, beating him toward the shut-
ters, leaping onto the window seat, and driving him back out into the
night. He was a sizeless, faceless creature to me. My son told me he was
blue, with big teeth.

This ritual went on for weeks. Sometimes, several times a night. I   6
continued my battle, and, as I tucked him back under the covers, I
explained that daddy would keep the monster from him always. I was
bigger and stronger; as long as I was there, no monster was going to
get my boy. I was wrong. No matter how hard I battled, the monster
returned when my son wanted him to. I was forced to accept the fact
that my macho approach to protecting him from his fears wasn't working. My dad never told me he would save me from my monsters. I
don't think he knew they existed.

As I thought back to my mummy and his eventual disappearance, I   7
realized that he had never really gone away. He was with me still. He
changed shapes as rapidly as I grew up. He became a wild bear at the
foot of my bed. Then, later, an amorphous flying object swooping over
my head. In later years, he was my first day at kindergarten, the agony
of my early attempts at the diving board. He was hurricanes and the
ocean, a mysterious death next door to us, my brother's ability to outdo
me in all sports. He was hypodermic needles, even early haircuts. Still
later, my first date, my first night away from home, at 16, alone in a
small boardinghouse as an apprentice in summer stock. The first
woman to say no, the first woman to say yes. And then, he became my
ambition, my fear of failure, struggles with success, marriage, husband-
hood, fatherhood. There's always a foot dragging somewhere in my
mind, it seems.

My son called out again. This time I went into his room, turned on   8
the light and sat down facing him. His eyes were wild with fear, wilder
than the earlier nights we had gone through this ritual. I asked him to
listen, but he couldn't hear me. He kept screaming and pointing at the
windows. "Kill him, kill him for me, daddy!" he cried. He grabbed the
pillow and tried to get me to do my routine. I felt I needed to speak to
him without the ritual's having happened first. When, at last, I could
quiet him, I said with trembling voice that I was never going to kill the
monster again. I explained that this was his monster. He had made him
up, and only he could kill him. I told him that the monster was in his
head and leapt out whenever he wanted him to. I said that he could
make him go away whenever he chose, or that he could turn him into a

friendly monster if he liked. He sat expressionless. He had never stared at me so hard. I said again that I would no longer perform this particular battle for him, but that I loved him and would always love him. A slow and overwhelmingly beautiful smile that I shall never forget came to his face and he said: "You mean, I can make him do anything I want?" "Yes," I said, "you're in charge of him."

I went back to bed and lay there waiting for the return of the monster. He didn't come back that night and has never again appeared in that form. Sometimes he's being driven from the living room by my son with his He-Man sword aloft, its scabbard stuck down the back of his pajamas as he cries out, "I am The Power." And sometimes he is under the covers in the big bed when the whole family plays tent. We just ask him, politely, to leave. He stays for dinner now and then. He's everything from 10 feet tall to a small tiny creature in the cup of my son's hand. He's blue, green, and sometimes he's a she.   9

As my son grows, I know we will be able to face his monsters together. And now, when all I was once so sure of has become a mystery to me, I'm hoping he'll be able to help me face the unknown ones yet to visit themselves upon me.   10

member that summer, the more I realize that there was no single *type* of worker. I am embarrassed to say I had not expected such diversity. I certainly had not expected to meet, for example, a plumber who was an abstract painter in his off hours and admired the work of Mark Rothko. Nor did I expect to meet so many workers with college diplomas. (They were the ones who were not surprised that I intended to enter graduate school in the fall.) I suppose what I really want to say here is painfully obvious, but I must say it nevertheless: the men of that summer were middle-class Americans. They certainly didn't constitute an oppressed society. Carefully completing their work sheets; talking about the fortunes of local football teams; planning Las Vegas vacations; comparing the gas mileage of various makes of campers—they were not *los pobres* my mother had spoken about.

On two occasions, the contractor hired a group of Mexican aliens. 10 They were employed to cut down some trees and haul off debris. In all, there were six men of varying age. The youngest in his late twenties; the oldest (his father?) perhaps sixty years old. They came and they left in a single old truck. Anonymous men. They were never introduced to the other men at the site. Immediately upon their arrival, they would follow the contractor's directions, start working—rarely resting—seemingly driven by a fatalistic sense that work which had to be done was best done as quickly as possible.

I watched them sometimes. Perhaps they watched me. The only 11 time I saw them pay me much notice was one day at lunchtime when I was laughing with the other men. The Mexicans sat apart when they ate, just as they worked by themselves. Quiet. I rarely heard them say much to each other. All I could hear were their voices calling out sharply to one another, giving directions. Otherwise, when they stood briefly resting, they talked among themselves in voices too hard to overhear.

The contractor knew enough Spanish, and the Mexicans—or at 12 least the oldest of them, their spokesman—seemed to know enough English to communicate. But because I was around, the contractor decided one day to make me his translator. (He assumed I could speak Spanish.) I did what I was told. Shyly I went over to tell the Mexicans that the *patrón* wanted them to do something else before they left for the day. As I started to speak, I was afraid with my old fear that I would be unable to pronounce the Spanish words. But it was a simple instruction I had to convey. I could say it in phrases.

The dark sweating faces turned toward me as I spoke. They 13 stopped their work to hear me. Each nodded in response. I stood there. I wanted to say something more. But what could I say in Spanish, even if I could have pronounced the words right? Perhaps I just wanted to engage them in small talk, to be assured of their confidence, our familiarity. I thought for a moment to ask them where in Mexico they were from. Something like that. And maybe I wanted to tell them (a lie, if need be) that my parents were from the same part of Mexico.

I stood there.   14

Their faces watched me. The eyes of the man directly in front of 15 me moved slowly over my shoulder, and I turned to follow his glance toward *el patrón* some distance away. For a moment I felt swept up by that glance into the Mexicans' company. But then I heard one of them returning to work. And then the others went back to work. I left them without saying anything more.

When they had finished, the contractor went over to pay them in 16 cash. (He later told me that he paid them collectively—"for the job," though he wouldn't tell me their wages. He said something quickly about the good rate of exchange "in their own country.") I can still hear the loudly confident voice he used with the Mexicans. It was the sound of the *gringo* I had heard as a very young boy. And I can still hear the quiet, indistinct sounds of the Mexican, the oldest, who replied. At hearing that voice I was sad for the Mexicans. Depressed by their vulnerability. Angry at myself. The adventure of the summer seemed suddenly ludicrous. I would not shorten the distance I felt from *los pobres* with a few weeks of physical labor. I would not become like them. They were different from me.

After that summer, a great deal—and not very much really— 17 changed in my life. The curse of physical shame was broken by the sun; I was no longer ashamed of my body. No longer would I deny myself the pleasing sensations of my maleness. During those years when middle-class black Americans began to assert with pride, "Black is beautiful," I was able to regard my complexion without shame. I am today darker than I ever was as a boy. I have taken up the middle-class sport of long-distance running. Nearly every day now I run ten or fifteen miles, barely clothed, my skin exposed to the California winter rain and wind or the summer sun of late afternoon. The torso, the soccer player's calves and thighs, the arms of the twenty-year-old I never was, I possess now in my thirties. I study the youthful parody shape in the mirror: the stomach lipped tight by muscle; the shoulders rounded by chin-ups; the arms veined strong. This man. A man. I meet him. He laughs to see me, what I have become.

The dandy. I wear double-breasted Italian suits and custom-made 18 English shoes. I resemble no one so much as my father—the man pictured in those honeymoon photos. At that point in life when he abandoned the dandy's posture, I assume it. At the point when my parents would not consider going on vacation, I register at the Hotel Carlyle in New York and the Plaza Athenée in Paris. I am as taken by the symbols of leisure and wealth as they were. For my parents, however, those symbols became taunts, reminders of all they could not achieve in one lifetime. For me those same symbols are reassuring reminders of public success. I tempt vulgarity to be reassured. I am filled with the gaudy delight, the monstrous grace of the nouveau riche.

In recent years I have had occasion to lecture in ghetto high 19 schools. There I see students of remarkable style and physical grace. (One can see more dandies in such schools than one ever will find in middle-class high schools.) There is not the look of casual assurance I saw students at Stanford display. Ghetto girls mimic high-fashion models. Their dresses are of bold, forceful color; their figures elegant, long; the stance theatrical. Boys wear shirts that grip at their over-developed muscular bodies. (Against a powerless future, they engage images of strength.) Bad nutrition does not yet tell. Great disappoint-ment, fatal to youth, awaits them still. For the moment, movements in school hallways are dancelike, a procession of postures in a sexual masque. Watching them, I feel a kind of envy. I wonder how different my adolescence would have been had I been free. . . . But no, it is my parents I see—their optimism during those years when they were en-tertained by Italian grand opera.

The registration clerk in London wonders if I have just been to 20 Switzerland. And the man who carries my luggage in New York guesses the Caribbean. My complexion becomes a mark of my leisure. Yet no one would regard my complexion the same way if I entered such hotels through the service entrance. That is only to say that my complexion assumes its significance from the context of my life. My skin, in itself, means nothing. I stress the point because I know there are people who would label me "disadvantaged" because of my color. They make the same mistake I made as a boy, when I thought a disad-vantaged life was circumscribed by particular occupations. That sum-mer I worked in the sun may have made me physically indistinguish-able from the Mexicans working nearby. (My skin was actually darker because, unlike them, I worked without wearing a shirt. By late August my hands were probably as tough as theirs.) But I was not one of *los pobres*. What made me different from them was an attitude of *mind*, my imagination of myself.

I do not blame my mother for warning me away from the sun 21 when I was young. In a world where her brother had become an old man in his twenties because he was dark, my complexion was some-thing to worry about. "Don't run in the sun," she warns me today. I run. In the end, my father was right—though perhaps he did not know how right or why—to say that I would never know what real work is. I will never know what he felt at his last factory job. If tomorrow I worked at some kind of factory, it would go differently for me. My long education would favor me. I could act as a public person—able to defend my interests, to unionize, to petition, to speak up—to challenge and demand. (I will never know what real work is.) I will never know what the Mexicans knew, gathering their shovels and ladders and saws.

Their silence stays with me now. The wages those Mexicans re-   22
ceived for their labor were only a measure of their disadvantaged condition. Their silence is more telling. They lack a public identity. They
remain profoundly alien. Persons apart. People lacking a union obviously, people without grounds. They depend upon the relative goodwill or fairness of their employers each day. For such people, lacking a
better alternative, it is not such an unreasonable risk.

Their silence stays with me. I have taken these many words to de-   23
scribe its impact. Only: the quiet. Something uncanny about it. Its compliance. Vulnerability. Pathos. As I heard their truck rumbling away, I
shuddered, my face mirrored with sweat. I had finally come face to
face with *los pobres*.

A Nigerian Looks at America

T. OBINKARAM ECHEWA

As a superannuated foreign student about to return to Nigeria 1
after more than twenty years in the United States, I feel ready to ven-
ture some answers to the question Americans have asked me hundreds
of times, namely: What do I think of their country?

To start, I must observe that both the country and I have changed 2
considerably in the time I have been here. When I first arrived as a
young man who grew up in rural eastern Nigeria, I found America an
enchanted garden and a magic shop. Over the years, as I became used
to the glitter, I found much that repulsed me and much to disagree
with. Then again, as I stayed longer, I matured to realize that America,
like every country, is a mixture of good and bad, with no monopoly on
virtue and wisdom as some Americans believe, or on vice and folly as
some detractors suggest.

American is prismatic and elusive. The picture that comes to my 3
mind when I reflect on it is not singular, uniform or coherent; it is not
a postcard landscape but a series of colorful splashes, a blinding psy-
chedelic light show.

As a song, America is a loud, discordant chant, a thousand disco 4
bands in an echo chamber, a series of outbursts—Pow! Whee! Ka-
zook!—like the text of a Batman or Superman cartoon.

Life in this country is crowded, frenetic, and breathless. Americans 5
loathe physical idleness the way nature is supposed to loathe a vacuum;
silence makes them equally uncomfortable.

Discipline

In temperament, America is young and hyperactive, unwilling and 6
unable to ponder deeply or at length. Americans apprehend rather
than comprehend ideas. They do not have the discipline or the en-
durance to wrap their minds around a thought. Instead they prefer to
grab, snatch, or make a stab at it. Their mental energies are usually
exerted as pulses rather than as continuously flowing force. Americans
tend to be direct and literal rather than allusive and figurative, stark
rather than subtle. They are happier dealing with statistics than with
nuances.

209

If America were a building it would be an office block or a sky- 7
scraper—a structure of steel, concrete, and glass, massive but without
curves or complication.

Detesting the ponderous, the complex, and the inconclusive, Amer- 8
icans simplify and abbreviate everything they come across. Even
"Hello" and "Goodbye" are shortened to "Hi" and "Bye." Some analysts
have suggested that America abandoned the Vietnam War effort simply because it became bored with its inconclusiveness.

In lieu of philosophers, modern America produces copywriters and 9
social scientists. American folk wisdom excludes anything that cannot
be placed on a poster or bumper sticker and read at a glance. Americans like an epigram or a catchy and alliterative jingle, with, if at all
possible, a sexually suggestive double-entendre.

American social and intellectual life is so bathed in clichés that it is 10
nearly impossible to think a fresh or original thought. Try to think in
America and your head swarms with ready-made phrases, stock expres-
sions, and instant, prepackaged ideas. These are continually belched
into the atmosphere like verbal exhaust and inhaled like smog by everyone who lives within the country's borders.

Then the fumes are repackaged, relabeled, and recirculated by 11
armies of new-idea hucksters—professional or self-anointed experts on
human behavior. To turn a quick profit, they market half-baked ideas,
grandiloquent pap, and pedestrian observations masquerading as science.

Americans are an inquisitive people, not inclined to leave anything 12
alone. If you give an American child a package, he will quickly tear off
the wrappings. If he finds a toy inside, he will start to play with it
immediately. He will play feverishly for a while and then discard the
toy out of boredom. Later, he might take it apart to see what makes it
go. By contrast, a traditionally reared African child is inclined to savor
the mystery of what is inside the package for some while. When he
eventually uncovers the toy, he will play with it only a little at a time, so
as not to use it up.

"That is why you Africans never made any progress," an American 13
friend said to me once when I made the above comparison. "You never
bothered to investigate the mysteries around you." Maybe.

It is true that one has to break an egg to make an omelet, but an 14
egg is much more than just an ingredient for an omelet. A fundamen-
tal danger that America poses to itself—and to a world it now domi-
nates—is its tendency to relegate every available egg to the making of
omelets.

Extremes

In the final analysis, Americans are merely human, though some of 15
my American friends bristle when lumped together with the rest of

mere humanity. What distinguishes America as a culture is the peculiar blend of human characteristics that are emphasized. Those traits usually touted in Fourth of July speeches—individualism, unrestrained freedom, competition—have served the country well up to a point. They are sometimes pursued to such extremes, however, that they end up vulgarizing human life and spirit.

Living successfully in modern America, no matter how or where 16 one chooses to live, can be like trying to hail a cab in Times Square after the theater on a rainy Saturday night: it demands more than a little Philistinism. The "American way of life" is not founded on the interplay of human virtues supporting and encouraging one another, but rather on competing human appetites keeping one another in check. America blunts one's finer sensibilities by insisting that life is a grabfest, a jungle, a dog-eat-dog fight.

All of the above notwithstanding, I have quite enjoyed my stay here 17 and obtained a good education. My criticisms apply mainly to American institutions rather than American people. As individuals Americans are kind, gracious, and very generous. To put it in cliché-ese, some of my best friends are Americans.

Thumbs Out

STEVE SPENCE

Each spring, I hope to see them again, hitchhiking on the roads 1
leading out of town, and each spring I feel a little older when I don't. I
keep an eye out for a kid who looks just a little like Bob Dylan, just a
guy going his own way, going against the grain of conformity, a kid
going off in search of something, or nothing.

I look for hitchhikers who read books while they wait for a ride. I 2
hope it's a book about Zen, or maybe Kerouac's *Dharma Bums*, or the
dreamy, mountain-top poetry of Gary Snyder. With pure envy, I scan
the destinations they've scrawled on pieces of cardboard: Key West!
Galveston! Frisco! Mexico! But I don't see them anymore.

Hitchhiking is about freedom, and a word you don't hear anymore: 3
bliss. Sometimes I lie awake at night remembering the way the night
sky looks in Arizona from the bed of a pickup. Once I saw Houston
appear on the horizon at dawn out the window of a '53 Chevy with a
southern sun coming up, a sun so big it gave me goosebumps. It was a
sun I'd never seen before nor would again, it was a moment never to be
repeated. Zen.

There was a girl behind the counter in a waffle shop in Odessa, 4
Texas, who I can still see clearly today, I will never stop missing her.
Ships passing in the night. If you told that girl you were hitching to
New Orleans just to see how that sun looks coming up on the Mississippi, or you were Chicago-bound because you just had to hear Dexter
Gordon live, she'd about faint with desire, you were a romantic man. A
girl once held my hand and walked with me all over the city of Port-
land, Oregon, on the strength of my having read her one Ferlinghetti
poem in a coffeehouse. Days of heaven.

In New Orleans, a bouncer named Jimmy Flood showed me a bub- 5
blegum card of himself to prove he had indeed been a contender, the
number-eight middleweight in the world, and then let me sleep on the
floor of his sad little room in the French Quarter, where many early
mornings I fell asleep to the infinitely heartsore sound of a tenor sax-
ophone drifting into the soft bayou air. Days I spent passing out Proc-
ter & Gamble soap samples, nights I spent at the ancient long bar of

212

Martin's, guzzling fifteen-cent beers and listening to lonesome old men, there was something so inscrutably fine about them. Over in the bars on Magazine Street, all sorts of classes were offered in sudden danger and serious immorality, two subjects not found on any college lists.

For 36 hours near Monahans, Texas, my thumb was shunned. 6 There had been a murder, sad to say the work of someone masquerading as a hitchhiker. I was considering a freight train nearby when a frizzy-haired fat lady in her sixties pulled up in a panel truck loaded with turnovers—thousands of turnovers!—which she had made and sold at road stops along U.S. 20. "He'p yesse'f, don't be bashful," she said. I ate four cherry ones and felt new again. In thanking her, I somehow mentioned the murder. She looked me square in the eyes and said, "Hail, don't waste yer life fussin' 'bout things like that, it don't make no never mind." Words burned into the memory, her face still so clear in my mind. A gift of living, no purchase necessary.

Another fat lady, this one in the white uniform of a hash house in 7 El Paso, warned me not to cross the bridge into Mexico (the toll was two cents). "Theyull *do you* that way," she whispered, making it sound kinky good. I should ask her along, I thought, I know a room in Chihuahua that goes for 35 cents a night. Okay, so there are no sheets, but right next door they make the most delicious pinto beans in a hot brothy stock for one dime, flour tortillas included. She was wrong, of course. Mexico is hitchhiker heaven, cheap and friendly and instructive, full of good poor people who got that way through no fault of their own, people who could survive hard times that would kill some folks in my own country. And they could still laugh.

Dropped off on the eastern edge of the Las Vegas strip once with a 8 dollar-fifty in my pocket, a ravenous hole in my gut and a cold night coming on, I stuck to the red line on the roulette table in four casinos and emerged on the western edge of town with twelve dollars in that pocket, two cheeseburgers in my belly and a six-pack in my duffel bag, ecstatic that I had enough left over for a $5 motel with TV. Now, *that was bliss*, I have never equaled that sense of exhilaration since, it was the moment I discovered just how much I loved this great vast country—because it was mine, *I owned it*. Donald Trump could own Manhattan and still never know how luxurious that bed felt.

Every town was different then. To a kid from Seattle, Galveston 9 was a mysterious foreign country. Malls and fast-food chains were still in the future, and television came with a total of three channels. No one knew the word "media."

Sometimes the cops would roust you from the park where you 10 slept. So you learned to sleep in graveyards, where cops never tread. Near Chopique, Louisiana, I awoke one dawn and thought I felt the tiniest thread of heat coming up from Jacques Lebeques six feet below, who'd been resting there for a century. What was your world like back then, Jacques?

The cops would check you out, sure, but they *always* let you go.   11
The ones in small towns even winked, wished you luck. And God bless the one in northern Idaho on a rainy spring night an eternity ago who let me sleep in a dry jail cell.

The only bad thing about hitchhiking is that it must end. And you   12
must come to accept, like everyone else, the treadmill of living, the tediousness of routine. And what would you pay now for the bliss you felt on seeing the skyline of San Francisco for the very first time?

Years later, I would find myself driving to work at some dorky   13
newspaper, dreading the thought of covering the dorky speaker at that day's dorky Businessmen's Club luncheon (good fellowship really meaning good business contacts), and I would pass the hitchhikers. And I wanted my freedom back so bad that I thought I *could* just pull over and abandon my life, and the road would welcome me back, the country would be mine again. To go nowhere in particular again. To see a place for the first time again. I wanted to write the tantalizing name on the cardboard, the name that makes me weak with yearning: Mexico! I wanted to jump out of the car and shout:

"Mexico, man, I'm going to Mexico! And if you don't think I'm goin', you   14
can count the days I'm gone!"

But I didn't.   15

PART SIX

Improving Your Writing

GETTING STARTED

Many students have trouble getting started writing, even after they have identified a topic that they want to write about. In talking with students about the problems of getting started, we learned how deeply frustrated some of them were. But we also were able to offer them some suggestions for overcoming the difficulties of putting their ideas on paper.

The most common problem is that many students believe that by identifying their topic—for example, "How Divorce Affects Children"—they have sufficient grounds for beginning to write. They start at once to look for an attention-grabbing opening sentence. Too often, unfortunately, the sentence that sounds fine in the writer's head loses some of its punch when it is transferred to paper. The usual solution is to scratch out that sentence and think of another, being sure to throw away the paper to destroy all traces of the false start. After discarding several attempts at an opening sentence, and filling the wastebasket with virtually unused paper, it's time for a snack, a short TV break, or a phone call. Later, the student returns to the drawing board to repeat this process in search of an elusive first sentence.

The trouble with this approach, apart from mounting frustration, is that the search for a good opening can divert your attention from your main goal, which is to express a particular *set of ideas* as effectively as possible. By itself, then, a good topic is seldom a sufficient basis for beginning to draft the essay.

From Topic to Thesis

Before trying to sum up your topic in a strong opening sentence, first you need to check your sense of direction. Decide what main idea, or *thesis*, you want to develop in the essay. Then, keep that general idea in mind as you jot down all the related ideas and examples that spring from it. By focusing on and expanding one major idea about your topic, you will get a fairly good sense of what you want to cover in your essay.

Selecting Your Thesis

Merely identifying a topic that you want to write about cannot provide the same degree of guidance that a thesis statement can, for a *thesis statement* goes beyond the topic and states the writer's point of view or attitude toward the topic. For example, if your topic is "How Divorce Affects Children," you might decide to emphasize the ideas expressed in the following thesis statement:

> Divorce seems to harm children between the ages of
>
> five and ten much more than it harms teenagers or
>
> infants.

Notice how this statement sets real boundaries for an essay. It establishes age groups for comparison, and it suggests that divorce affects these groups differently. Now the writer should have little difficulty planning the essay, since the thesis statement calls for a description of the harmful effects of divorce on each age group. This naturally leads the writer to give evidence or state a theory that accounts for the differences described. The writer can move confidently to the next step, which is to organize this series of ideas into an effective outline for the essay.

Sometimes it is difficult to select a thesis. For example, you may disagree strongly with one of the readings in this book or with an opinion expressed by a classmate. Merely stating that you disagree, however, does not indicate the path that your own thoughts will take in the essay. To map out your course, we recommend that you try a technique called *brainstorming,* in which you quickly list any and all ideas that come to mind as you consider your topic. Do not censor yourself, saying "Oh, that's silly" or "It won't work" or "That doesn't fit my earlier response." Let *all* your thoughts flow freely for about five or ten minutes. Then, relax and look over the list to see whether any pattern appears. When you let down your guard this way, it often happens that your thoughts tend to veer in a particular direction, and you will see a thesis emerging from them.

Brainstorming is a bit like the practice of searching for a strong first sentence, except that you just jot down ideas and you *don't* discard all your false starts. Instead, you set aside a period of time in which you suspend all judgment and simply list every idea you have, no matter how unimportant it may seem. Surprisingly, many of the ideas will be related. When your brainstorming period is over and you consider the results as a whole, you will probably find a set of related ideas that suggest a thesis statement to guide your essay.

Remember that an important aspect of selecting your thesis is to consider your audience and your purpose for writing. The reading and responding process used in this book helps you to understand your audience, since you get feedback from other students when you share your initial response to an essay. During drafting, too, the reactions of your classmates can tell you whether or not you are reaching your audience effectively. Their comments also can help you define the purpose of your writing. Do you want to inform them about something, or do you hope to persuade them to agree with you? Their reactions to your ideas will tell you whether you are achieving your purpose. By considering your audience and how you want your writing to affect them, you will discover which ideas you want to emphasize in your thesis statement.

Stating Your Thesis

Merely saying that you disagree with someone ties you to that person's ideas. Your essay will be more interesting and original if you first make a positive statement that expresses your own ideas about the topic.

For example, about half of our students responded to Gordon Liddy's piece, "Without Emotion" (see Part One), by writing something like this: "I think Liddy was [wrong] [crazy] [evil] [foolish] to practice killing without emotion." But students who moved beyond mere judgments of Liddy to make strong personal statements found it easier to write solid, interesting essays. Here are some of their thesis statements:

```
Soldiers who suppress their sympathy for other

people's suffering become machines, just like the Nazis

did in Germany.


It's foolish to think you can train yourself not to

feel compassion for your fellow human beings, because at

some point you'll fall apart emotionally.


Killing innocent creatures is evil because it leads

people to think murder and war are reasonable ways to

solve problems.
```

Besides making it easier to write an effective essay, thesis statements like these result in essays that can stand alone. Readers do not have to know the passage from Liddy's book; they can react directly to the ideas presented in the essay.

Developing Your Thesis

By considering your audience, purpose, and topic, you have selected and stated a thesis. Now you need to gather and organize ideas to support your thesis. Again, the technique of brainstorming will help; set aside a few minutes in which you list all the ideas that come to mind without judging them. When the ideas stop flowing, take a deep breath and examine each item on your list. Does the first item relate in any way to your thesis statement? If it doesn't, cross it out, and move to the second item on your list. Examine each of your ideas in terms of your thesis statement. If you are writing about the effects of divorce on young children and teenagers, you can cross out any idea that doesn't fit—such as the legal aspects of divorce, or the high cost of a lawyer. Use your thesis statement to guide you in deciding which ideas support your point of view and which ideas are unimportant.

When you have crossed out all the unimportant ideas on your list, study the ideas that remain, and begin to explore them further. At this point you might like to try *freewriting*—write a few sentences about each item on your list, again without judging the results. For a brief period of time, let your ideas flow. If one sentence leads to another, go with it; find out where it leads. After freewriting, look over your sentences and group them into related ideas (for example, group all the sentences about divorce and young children). In this way you will develop a rough outline of ideas and details to support your thesis.

Drafting the Essay

After you have stated your thesis and have developed and outlined your ideas about it, you are ready to undertake the sentence-by-sentence writing of the essay. Although the problem of getting started has been resolved by first stating a thesis and preparing a rough outline of supporting ideas and details, you may still find yourself crumpling up sheets of paper to discard less-than-wonderful opening sentences. Many people seem to feel that almost anything they write is not good enough. Even if they get past the first sentence, the second or third one has them crossing out and discarding their efforts.

To avoid all this frustration, our advice is to write your first draft uncritically, without concern for the quality of your word choices and sentence structure. As you did during brainstorming and freewriting, write rapidly, just to record your ideas on paper, where they won't get lost (as they surely will if you struggle over every word and sentence in a quest for perfection).

"Writer's block"—the inability to write anything at all—often results from fear of failure. But no failure is possible during the drafting phase, since you alone will be the reader. So don't be too critical as you begin drafting. Wait until your first draft is finished before examining its content, organization, mechanics, grammar, and style.

Besides the danger of writer's block, another pitfall of trying to write a "perfect" first draft is that you are likely to lose sight of the thesis itself. Your main idea may then become just one of several ideas that seem equally important, leaving readers to wonder what you hoped to accomplish in your essay. Following is an example of how an introductory paragraph can go astray when the writer pays more attention to sentence structure and grammar than to the ideas he or she wants to express. Notice that each sentence is clear and well written; yet no main idea emerges:

> In the beginning of the world, when God made the animals and placed Adam and Eve in charge of them, all the Earth's creatures lived together in peace. Things are different now. Hunting and fishing have become big sports because many people think animals were put on Earth just for their pleasure. And some scientists torture and even kill animals for "the advancement of civilization!" I gave up eating meat when I became old enough to realize how the meat came to my dinner plate. Some animals do serve a useful purpose, but the rest exist in Nature, just being their beautiful selves. No one should ever kill these animals, for they have just as much right to life as we do. I belong to several organizations that are working to stop the cruel killing of animals. But the government does little to help them. How can we call ourselves civilized if we keep on killing innocent creatures?

This paragraph goes off in so many directions that it does not point clearly in any particular direction. We can tell that the writer is fond of animals and believes that human beings abuse them in many ways. And if we have read "Without Emotion," we may also sense that the essay is a response to Gordon Liddy's writing. However, the writer has not focused on one specific statement about how people abuse animals. This relatively short essay cannot tackle all the problems at once. Yet the introductory paragraph mentions hunting as a sport, research experiments, slaughterhouses, and commercial hunting of endangered species. Each of these examples of killing leads to different arguments against them, even though all are linked by a common humanitarian point of view. Moreover, each category of abuse can be treated by the writer as a social problem, as a moral issue, or as a scientific matter.

To clear up the confusion and focus the essay, the writer's specific topic and point of view must both be spelled out in the form of a thesis statement early in the essay. This would guide both the readers and the writer, who at this point is trying to draft a well-organized piece of writing.

After a conference with the instructor, this student determined what the strongest topic was and from that developed a thesis statement. What most troubled the student was the commercial hunting of animals in order to use parts of their bodies—not for essential food but for vain, frivolous ends, such as fur coats, fancy shoes, cosmetics, and aphrodisiacs. The main purpose of the essay, therefore, would be to convince readers to join the crusade against slaughtering wild animals for profit.

Next, the student drafted two fairly different opening paragraphs and read both to the class for reaction. Of the following two paragraphs, which one do you think has a stronger thesis and thus would lead to a better essay?

Last month my father received an appeal from

Greenpeace, a worldwide environmental protection

society, asking him to send money to help them stop the

killing of whales and other endangered species. Dad

threw the letter down and complained about all the junk

mail we get. I told him this letter was not "junk"; these

people are hoping to save innocent and beautiful

creatures from extinction. I offered to donate some of

my allowance if he would contribute the same amount.

Eventually I convinced him that killing all these

animals is a crime against Nature, like hunting the

passenger pigeon to extinction a hundred years ago. I
have earned a reputation at school as a conservation
freak, but my work has raised a lot of money for
conservation groups. And our conservation club at
school is now working hard to convince the government to
help preserve all living things on our planet.

We Americans have done a good deal for conservation,
but a lot more remains to be done to protect Nature
against all the greedy people who do not respect our
wildlife. Ever since I was a Girl Scout, I have been
concerned with animal welfare. At first, I was busy
saving dogs hit by cars and curing wounded birds and
animals I found in the woods. I didn't know about
hunters who viciously slaughter whales and seals, or
African poachers who kill elephants, rhinos, and
gorillas for profit. When I learned about these awful
things, I helped start a club that raises money and sets
up protest marches in order to get our government to
protect the future of our planet. My life's goal is to
educate everyone to the danger and the immorality of
killing rare and beautiful animals who have the same
right as humans to live their lives in peace.

In using the reading and responding approach, be careful to distinguish between (1) writing a response, (2) brainstorming and freewriting, and (3) drafting the essay. The first step allows you to discover an interesting topic. The second step opens your mind and helps you to gather information related to your topic. The last step must be based solidly on the first two, developing in full your main idea about the topic. A well-formed thesis statement is the key to writing a successful first draft.

REVISING YOUR FIRST DRAFT

Every writer wishes that the first draft could be the last draft. Writing is difficult work, and the work never really ends because a word, sentence, paragraph, or essay can always be revised one more time. In addition, the elements and procedures of writing are intertwined: As you begin outlining your ideas, you also probably think about choosing the right word and even about spelling it correctly; or, as you look over your writing to check the spelling and grammar, you may suddenly realize that the essay is not organized as logically as you thought. Finally, when you write something, you *know* what you mean, and it may be difficult for you to see that other people—your readers—may not understand you. That's why we encourage you to share your early responses and first drafts with your classmates. Their questions and suggestions will help you to discover which aspects of your writing need revision.

Even the best writers know that revision is unavoidable, and they welcome the help of readers and editors along the way to their final draft. Whether you are an expert speller and grammarian or a writer who needs constantly to consult a dictionary and a handbook, "correctness" is only one part of effective writing—and only one part of effective revision. The main goal of writing is to express your point of view convincingly, and that should be your first concern in revising. Did you make yourself clear? Did your readers understand your main point and what you think about it? Was the information in your essay arranged logically and conveyed in effective language? When readers say "yes" to those three questions, you can be satisfied that revision is almost at an end. *Then* it's time to focus on the appearances of writing. Do the sentences in a paragraph flow smoothly? Is each sentence grammatical? Is each word spelled correctly? Finally, is your handwriting or typing neat and legible, so that the physical look of the essay doesn't distract readers from what you are saying?

Revision, then, is always possible, often necessary, and usually beneficial to your writing. To illustrate this point, the following pages present two examples of how students revised their essays after receiving written comments. Example 1 shows how an instructor's comments helped the student to revise, and Example 2 shows a revision based on a classmate's comments. As you study the first drafts, the comments, and the revised drafts, notice how these writers improved the expression of their ideas by taking readers' suggestions into account.

Example 1

First Draft

Misplaced Kindness

At first the story of how Mrs. Brown helped Mary
made me feel good because I enjoy reading about kind
people. But then I began to think about the other
students in Mrs. Brown's class who also needed help.
Maybe they were not as needy as Mary, but they could have
used some extra attention to make them good students
instead of just average ones. When a teacher spends too
much time and energy on the losers, the rest of the
students have to improve all by themselves. Most of them
cannot do it alone, and so that means Mrs. Brown was not
a good example of a perfect teacher.

Many of the students in my classes were like Mary in
some way or another, and most of the teachers especially
in grade school gave extra time to these "difficult"
students. That meant that the rest of us had to sit
around very bored, or else we fooled around, while those
teachers played Mommy to misbehaving children or those
who did not really care about school. I resented the
fact that these teachers did not help me to do better in
math and science, my worst enemies.

The writer wants us to believe that Mrs. Brown's
efforts paid off in a big way for Mary, but I would not
bet any money on how well Mary ever did as a result of all

that love and TLC. Some of the students in my classes who received extra attention are now unable to hold a job. What good did that special treatment do them? Furthermore, most of those losers never really wanted the extra help; they just did not dare refuse it. But the worst part of all this is that some of my friends who barely managed to pass are now running into trouble as they try to handle college work. If that extra help had gone to them, they would have made good use of it and would not be struggling to survive now.

I think that the article was meant to make teachers feel guilty if they are not giving all of themselves to their students, especially those at the bottom. This writer thinks she knows what is best, but she really does not understand the students. Doesn't she realize that most dropouts just plain do not like school? All they want to do is hang out. They actually resent teachers meddling in their personal lives. My advice to the teachers of the world is to concentrate on those who can really use their help. Let the losers stay lost.

Instructor's Comments about First Draft

Paragraph 1: Try to be more direct in your first sentence. What did you *think* of what Mrs. Brown did?

Can you be more specific about the other students' neediness? Your readers need to know what conditions you are focusing on. State your thesis more forcefully to express your point of view.

In last sentence, reconsider your word choice. The author never said that Mrs. Brown was *perfect*.

Paragraph 2: What do you mean by "we fooled around"? It doesn't add much to your point, and it makes the sentence a bit long and awkward. If you have details to add here, develop them more fully; readers won't know what you mean.

In the last sentence, it would help readers to know the extent of your difficulties in math and science. Did you fail these courses? What could the teachers of these courses have done to make you do better? Better than *what*?

Paragraph 3: The first sentence is too informal to tell us much, and the use of *TLC* assumes that readers will know what this term means. Express these ideas more clearly.

The entire paragraph covers too much ground. It has no single main idea. Finish your prediction of Mary's future before you discuss weak students you have known. Then, devote yet another paragraph to your friends in college. You cover too many ideas, but readers don't get a clear idea of what you mean.

Last paragraph: I think you are too harsh in judging the author. Don't forget that your first impression was highly favorable, as you say in the very first sentence of your essay. Tone down your criticism, and, if it seems reasonable, give Mrs. Brown a little credit. Did she do anything that you approve of?

Toward the end of the essay, take another look at your word choices. (1) You are not referring only to "dropouts." (2) Avoid slang phrases like "hang out"—try to be more formal to reach a wider audience. (3) In the last sentence, "really use" is vague and conversational; almost everyone can "really use" help, and so your conclusion is weakened by this phrase.

Entire essay: I found your essay very effective. Although I tend to agree with the author regarding Mrs. Brown's strategy with Mary, your essay showed me why it is so hard for most teachers to follow her example. They probably share your view to some extent.

Revised Draft

Misplaced Kindness

At first I agreed that Mrs. Brown was an excellent teacher because I felt sorry for Mary. But then I began to think about the other students in Mary's class who also needed help. They may not have repeated first grade and may not have been troublemakers, but they could have used extra attention to enable them to become good students rather than just average ones. When a teacher spends too much time and energy on the losers, the rest of the students have to improve on their own. And since most students cannot do this, they remain weak and may even lose interest in school. The more I thought about this story, the more I became convinced that Mrs. Brown was not an outstanding teacher.

When I was going to school, many of my classes contained students who were like Mary in one way or another, and most of the teachers, especially in grade school, gave extra time to these "problem" students. That meant that the rest of us had to sit around very bored, while these teachers played "mommy" to misbehaving children who were not really interested in school in the first place. When I had trouble getting even a C in math and science, I resented seeing teachers giving their time to students who usually failed anyway and did not care at all about learning.

This writer wants us to believe that Mrs. Brown's efforts were very beneficial to Mary, but I feel certain that Mary did not do any better because of all this love and attention. She probably went back to her old ways as soon as she left Mrs. Brown's class. Other teachers would not spend so much time trying to improve Mary's self-image, and she would soon be misbehaving in order to get attention or because she felt inferior to the other children.

Most weak students do poorly because they are not interested in school subjects, and they have no ambition. Some of the people in my classes who received a lot of extra help over the years are now unable to find a job. What good did all that special treatment do for them? Furthermore, most of those losers never really wanted the extra help; they did not dare refuse it.

But the worst part of all is that some of my friends who barely managed to pass high school are now running into trouble as they try to handle college work. If more of that extra assistance for Mary had been given to them, they could have made good use of it and would not be struggling to survive now.

The writer intended to make teachers feel guilty if they were not giving all of themselves to those students who are having the greatest difficulty. What she says sounds nice because Mrs. Brown is so kind and Mary's behavior does improve. But the writer does not realize that most poor students just plain don't like school. All they want to do is hang out with their friends. They resent teachers meddling in their personal lives. My advice to teachers is to concentrate on those who can make the best use of their assistance. Let the losers stay lost.

This student read the instructor's comments before revising the first draft. As you can see, some of the revisions were based on the instructor's guidance, while others came from the student as part of the revision process.

1. How closely did the student follow the instructor's advice in revising the first draft? Which suggestions did the student accept, and which were rejected?
2. Which changes in the revised draft came from the student without the advice of the instructor? Do you think the student's revisions improved the essay? Why or why not?
3. In what way is the revised draft more effective than the first draft? Be specific in noting which ideas were improved by revision.

Example 2

First Draft

A Young Woman in Big Trouble

My own adolescence had its ups and downs, but for
the most part I enjoyed growing up. Maybe things went
well for me because I moved ahead at a normal pace, and I
got along pretty well with my parents most of the time.
On the other hand, my fourteen-year-old sister, Joann,
seems to be having a very rough time. She hardly speaks
to Mom and Dad, and she has fallen in with a wild bunch
who are always getting into trouble of one kind or
another. I wish some understanding person could see
Joann's need for help and find some way to reach out to
her. I believe Joann's tough attitude is just her way of
keeping her personal pain hidden from the world.
Somebody outside our family must get through to her
before she wrecks her life.

Joann's problem goes back a long way. She came along
when I was seven and my older sister Clare was nine.
Mother had gone back to her job as a pediatric nurse and
did not want to return to the role of housewife/mother.
So babysitters were hired to care for Joann until she
was old enough to go to kindergarten. None of them
stayed very long. When I think back about Joann as a
small child, I see a sour-faced brat, whose tears and
shouts seemed fake about half the time.

School solved the babysitting problem because

Clare and I could be assigned that job when we came home from school. I resented having to look after Joann, and I probably took my frustration out on her some of the time. Then she hit sixth grade, and everything changed.

When Joann, who wins the prize for good looks in our family, turned twelve, she became popular in school for the first time. Not with the teachers--she has never done well on report cards, especially in "attitude"-- but with those girls who dress like Brooke Shields and act like they are eighteen. When Mother saw Joann's rapid transformation, she began criticizing her behavior, instead of just complaining as we had all been doing for years. Clare and I felt our parents were being a bit hard on Joann, but we were not worried then because we had fought with them about those things ourselves.

Recently, it became clear to us that the group of girls Joann hangs out with are even more rebellious than we had thought. They spend their afternoons and weekends with guys who are much older and wilder than is good for someone Joann's age. When Clare and I try to talk to Joann about the situation, she will not listen. She tells us to mind our own business.

Since I cannot see Joann responding to any of us, I desperately hope that someone she can respect will come along and take note of her troubled condition. She needs a true friend, and soon!

Classmate's Comments about First Draft

Paragraph 1: The way you begin seems wrong somehow—you're talking about *your* life, not your sister's, and it doesn't have much to do with her, either.

What kind of trouble was your sister "always getting into"? I know the teacher told us not to go into too much detail in our introductions, but she also said to be sure that readers know what you're getting at. I thought the trouble might be drugs at first—and you do mention that later—but I wasn't sure when I read the first paragraph.

The last half of the paragraph jumps around too much. You want someone to help Joann; then you explain her attitude; then you come back to wanting someone outside the family to help her. I think the last idea is a good way to end this paragraph, but you need to tell me why no one in the family can help. Give a clearer picture of her problem before you say what you think has to happen if she's going to get better.

Paragraph 2: I think the last sentence should go at the beginning, just after the first sentence.

Paragraph 3: You could say more about Joann—how she acted, how she must have felt.

Paragraph 4: I like the way you describe Joann and her friends. But why did your mother criticize her? What did she do wrong, other than act like a movie star? And what did your parents dislike about the other girls? What "issues" did they fight about?

Paragraph 5: What was so wild about these kids? What do you mean by "much older"—in their twenties?

What about your talks with Joann? What goes wrong? I think you need another paragraph to describe the way she turns off to you, and I think these two paragraphs should go up near the beginning of the essay so we can get a better idea of how much trouble Joann is in.

Last Paragraph: This conclusion seems weak to me. You just sign off with a prayer for divine assistance. Why not go into more detail about the communication problem before you ask for an outsider to help your sister?

Revised Draft

A Young Woman in Big Trouble

My fourteen-year-old sister Joann seems to be
having a very rough time growing up. She hardly ever
speaks to Mom and Dad, and she and her friends have
fallen in with an older group of guys who are always in
trouble of one kind or another. Joann had an unhappy

childhood and has developed a tough attitude to keep her
personal pain hidden from the world. None of us can get
through to her, and so I keep praying that she finds
someone she can trust who will straighten her out before
she completely wrecks her life.

Joann's problem goes back a long way. She was born
when I was seven and my sister Clare was nine. When I
think back about Joann as a small child, I always see a
sour-faced brat whose tears and shouts seemed fake about
half the time. At the time I hated her for being so bad
tempered. But looking back now, I can see that she
probably felt unwanted because no one in the family paid
much attention to her unless she was making a very loud
noise.

Mother had gone back to her job as a pediatric nurse
after I started school, and she did not want to return to
the role of housewife. So she hired babysitters for
Joann until she was old enough for kindergarten. None of
them stayed very long, and this may have left Joann
feeling insecure. When she began going to school, Clare
and I became the babysitters. However, this didn't help
Joann, for I resented having to take care of her, and I
took my frustration out on her some of the time. Clare
was not much better. So the next six years weren't much
better for Joann than the first six. Then she hit
seventh grade, and everything changed dramatically.

When Joann, who wins the prize for good looks in our
family, turned twelve, she became popular in school for
the first time. Not with the teachers--she has never
done well on report cards, especially in "attitude." She

began hanging out with those girls who dress like Brooke Shields and act like they are eighteen. When Mother saw how Joann was changing, she began criticizing her behavior, including the way she dressed and her use of makeup. Both Mom and Dad were very critical of Joann's friends, who used foul language and hung around with a rough bunch of boys.

At first, Clare and I thought our parents were being too tough on Joann, and we were not worried about her because we had fought with our parents about similar issues ourselves. But recently, it became clear to us that the girls Joann goes around with are even more rebellious than we had thought. They spend their afternoons and weekends with guys who are much older than they are. Some have dropped out of high school, and all of them are involved with drugs and liquor.

When Clare and I try to talk to Joann about the situation, she will not listen. She tells us that she knows what she is doing and that she is in full control of her life. According to her, Clare and I missed out on all the excitement that is waiting for people who are brave enough to ignore all the myths that parents invent to control their children. Joann thinks our concern for her just shows how much we envy all the freedom she enjoys.

Mom and Dad have totally lost control of the situation. They cannot speak to Joann about anything without causing anger on both sides, and so they try to avoid her. Clare has very little time, for she is married and lives across town. So I am the only one who regularly talks to Joann, and then I can't mention the

problems, or else she quickly tunes me out. I feel so

terribly frustrated, having to stand by and watch my

sister destroy her life this way. I guess we are all to

blame--Mom and Dad for leaving her alone, and Clare and

I for treating her like a bratty sister all those years.

I just hope and pray it is not too late and that she can

find a true friend who will get her to realize what is

happening before she ends up in very serious trouble.

In this case, the student revised the first draft in response to a classmate's comments; the instructor made no suggestions at all.

1. What do you think of the classmate's comments? Were they as helpful as the instructor's comments were in Example 1? When you respond to a classmate's writing, are your comments as good as these? What can you learn from this classmate's response to the first draft?
2. Which of the classmate's comments would you have followed, and which would you have ignored? Why?
3. Look again at the first draft. What suggestions would you make to this writer? Put your comments in a form like the classmate's in this example. How would you advise this writer to proceed in revising the first draft?

A CHECKLIST FOR READING, RESPONDING, AND WRITING

Reading

Whether you are reading an assignment in this book or a classmate's first draft of an essay:

1. Relax and let your thoughts run free during your first reading.
2. Don't analyze what you are reading. Accept it—for now.
3. Pay attention to the ideas and feelings that you have as you read.

Responding to Reading

When you first respond to a reading selection or to a classmate's draft:

1. Record your strongest ideas and feelings about it without concern for the author's intentions or your instructor's expectations.
2. Record your response as soon as you finish reading the selection.
3. Share your response, either in class or as instructed.

Writing

After sharing your initial response with classmates, ask yourself the following questions to develop your thesis and draft your essay:

Selecting and Developing the Thesis

1. What point do I want to make about my topic? What do I hope to achieve? What does my audience know about the topic?
2. Is my topic focused enough, or do I need to limit it further?
3. Is my thesis clear and specific? Will my readers understand which aspects of the topic interest me and what my point of view is?
4. Should I use freewriting to develop my thesis further? Do I know all the ideas I want to explore in proving my point?
5. Do I need a classmate's reaction to my ideas at this point?

235

Drafting the Essay

1. Am I ready to start writing? Should I use brainstorming and freewriting to develop my ideas further?
2. Given my purpose and audience, how should I state my thesis in the introductory paragraph?
3. What is the best way to organize my supporting ideas and examples?
4. How should I state my conclusions in the last paragraph?
5. Can I improve the flow of ideas from thesis to supporting details to conclusion? Will my readers be able to follow my thinking?
6. Is my first draft ready for the instructor or classmates to read?

Responding to Writing

When you comment on a classmate's writing, questions like the following will help make your criticism constructive:

1. Do I agree or disagree with what the author is saying?
2. If I agree with the author's thesis, could I present the case any better? What other ideas would I include to support this thesis?
3. If I disagree with the author's thesis, what is the strongest case I can build against it? What ideas would I offer to support my objections?
4. What ideas can I offer to make this essay more effective?

Revising the Essay

After your instructor or classmates have reacted to your first draft of an essay, ask yourself these questions:

1. What comments did my readers offer that I want to consider in revising the essay? Which of their comments should I ignore?
2. Did my readers understand my thesis and feel that my supporting details and conclusions fit my thesis? Which ideas do I need to expand or clarify? Which ideas should I drop from the essay?
3. Did my readers object to any of the word choices I made?
4. Are all the sentences grammatically correct? Do they flow smoothly within each paragraph?
5. Have I made any mistakes in spelling, punctuation, or capitalization?
6. Am I ready to revise the essay and copy it neatly, or do I need further reaction from the instructor or classmates?

"What's in a Name? Quite a Lot," by Lois Sweet. Reprinted with permission—the Toronto Star Syndicate.

"How Cocaine Took Control of My Life," by Tony Elliott. Copyright 1986 by the New York Times Company. Reprinted by permission.

Excerpt from *Television: The Plug-in Drug* by Marie Winn. Copyright 1977, 1985 by Marie Winn Miller. Used by permission of Viking Penguin, a division of Penguin Books USA Inc.

"Punishment versus Discipline," from *A Good Enough Parent* by Bruno Bettleheim. Copyright 1987 by Bruno Bettleheim. Reprinted by permission of Alfred A. Knopf, Inc.

Excerpt from *The Mirages of Marriage* by William J. Lederer and Don D. Jackson, M.D., by permission of W. W. Norton & Company, Inc. Copyright 1968 by W. W. Norton & Company, Inc.

"The Pursuit of Loneliness" from *The Pursuit of Loneliness* by Philip E. Slater. Copyright 1970, 1976 by Philip E. Slater. Reprinted by permission of Beacon Press.

"Males Just Born Gross—Humor Them," by Stephanie Brush. First appeared in the *Arizona Republic* (August 13, 1990).

"The Darkness After," by Ed & Lorraine Warren with Robert David Chase. Copyright 1989 by Ed & Lorraine Warren with Robert David Chase. From the book *Ghost Hunters* and used with permission from St. Martin's Press, Inc., New York, NY.

"How to Stay Alive," by Art Hoppe. Copyright the San Francisco Chronicle. Reprinted by permission.

"The Monsters in My Head," by Frank Langella. Copyright 1986 by the New York Times Company. Reprinted by permission.

"Labor" from *Hunger of Memory* by Richard Rodriguez. Copyright 1982 by Richard Rodriguez. Reprinted by permission of David R. Godine, Publisher.

"A Nigerian Looks at America," by T. Obinkaram Echewa. Copyright T. Obinkaram Echewa. Reprinted by permission.

"Thumbs Out," by Steve Spence. Copyright 1991 by Steve Spence, Car and Driver Magazine. Reprinted by permission.

GUIDE TO AUTHORS AND TITLES

Ashton-Warner, Sylvia, *Rolf*, 53
Asimov, Isaac, *Intelligence*, 104

Bartlett, Arthur, *Your Eyes Can Deceive You*, 92
Bayan, Gregory, *Reflections on a Hockey Helmet*, 122
Bettelheim, Bruno, *Punishment versus Discipline*, 184
Boy Who Drew Cats, The (Hearn), 135
Brush, Stephanie, *Males Just Born Gross—Humor Them*, 193

Chekhov, Anton, *The Slanderer*, 63
Children's Insults (Farb), 154
Chopin, Kate, *The Story of an Hour*, 100
Condon, John C., Jr., *Saying It May Make It So*, 167
Cosby, Bill, *A Fling on the Track*, 47

Darkness After, The (Warren and Warren with Chase), 195

Echewa, T. Obinkaram, *A Nigerian Looks at America*, 209
Elliott, Tony, *How Cocaine Took Control of My Life*, 176

Farb, Peter, *Children's Insults*, 154
Father (Hughes), 59
Ferraro, Susan, *Small-fry Swearing*, 140
Fling on the Track, A (Cosby), 47
Frank, Francine, and Frank Anshen, *Talking Like a Lady: How Women Talk*, 162
Fulbright, Evelyn R., *Mary and Mrs. Brown*, 8
Fulghum, Robert, *Good News*, 42

Gibbs, Angelica, *The Test*, 169
Good News (Fulghum), 42
Growing Up in the Shadow of an Older Brother or Sister (Helgesen), 97

Hearn, Lafcadio, *The Boy Who Drew Cats*, 135
Helgesen, Sally, *Growing Up in the Shadow of an Older Brother or Sister*, 97
Henri (Orwell), 58
Hoppe, Art, *How to Stay Alive*, 198
How about Low-cost Drugs for Addicts? (Nizer), 128
How Cocaine Took Control of My Life (Elliott), 176
How Fathers Talk to Babies (McLaughlin), 164
How to Stay Alive (Hoppe), 198
Hughes, Langston, *Father*, 55; *Salvation*, 77

Intelligence (Asimov), 104

Kupfer, Fern, *A Real Loss*, 87
Kushner, Harold, *What Makes Things Wrong?*, 117

Labor (Rodriguez), 203
Langella, Frank, *The Monsters in My Head*, 200
Lederer, William J., and Donald D. Jackson, *The Mirages of Marriage*, 188
Liddy, G. Gordon, *Without Emotion*, 36
Lorenz, Konrad, *The Young and the Old*, 133

Males Just Born Gross—Humor Them (Brush), 193
Mary and Mrs. Brown (Fulbright), 8

McLaughlin, Barry, *How Fathers Talk to Babies*, 164

Mirages of Marriage, The (Lederer and Jackson), 188

Mitchell, Richard, *Words as Weapons*, 147

Monsters in My Head, The (Langella), 200

Morris, Willie, *Our English Teacher*, 61

Nigerian Looks at America, A (Echewa), 209

Nizer, Louis, *How about Low-cost Drugs for Addicts?*, 128

No Allusions in the Classroom (O'Neill), 110

O'Neill, Jaime M., *No Allusions in the Classroom*, 110

Orwell, George, *Henri*, 58

Our English Teacher (Morris), 61

Parallel Speaking and Real Conversation (Rubin), 158

Peck, M. Scott, *Problems and Pain*, 131

Problems and Pain (Peck), 131

Punishment versus Discipline (Bettelheim), 184

Pursuit of Loneliness, The (Slater), 190

Real Loss, A (Kupfer), 87

Reflections on a Hockey Helmet (Bayan), 122

Reichl, Ruth, *There's Only Luck*, 94

Rodriguez, Richard, *Labor*, 203

Rolf (Ashton-Warner), 53

Rubin, Theodore Isaac, *Parallel Speaking and Real Conversation*, 158

Salvation (Hughes), 75

Saying It May Make It So (Condon), 167

Slanderer, The (Chekhov), 63

Slater, Philip, *The Pursuit of Loneliness*, 190

Small-fry Swearing (Ferraro), 140

Spence, Steve, *Thumbs Out*, 212

Stanton, Elizabeth Cady, *You Should Have Been a Boy!*, 68

Story of an Hour, The (Chopin), 100

Sweet, Lois, *What's in a Name?*, 174

Talking Like a Lady; How Women Talk (Frank and Anshen), 162

Television: The Plug-in Drug (Winn), 179

Test, The (Gibbs), 169

There's Only Luck (Reichl), 94

Thoele, Sue Patton, *Unresolved Grief: Drowning in Life's Debris*, 81

Thumbs Out (Spence), 212

Unresolved Grief: Drowning in Life's Debris (Thoele), 81

Warren, Ed and Lorraine, with Robert David Chase, *The Darkness After*, 195

What Makes Things Wrong? (Kushner), 117

What's in a Name? (Sweet), 174

Winn, Marie, *Television: The Plug-in Drug*, 179

Without Emotion (Liddy), 36

Words as Weapons (Mitchell), 147

You Should Have Been a Boy! (Stanton), 6

Your Eyes Can Deceive You (Bartlett), 92

Young and the Old, The (Lorenz), 133